Orkney

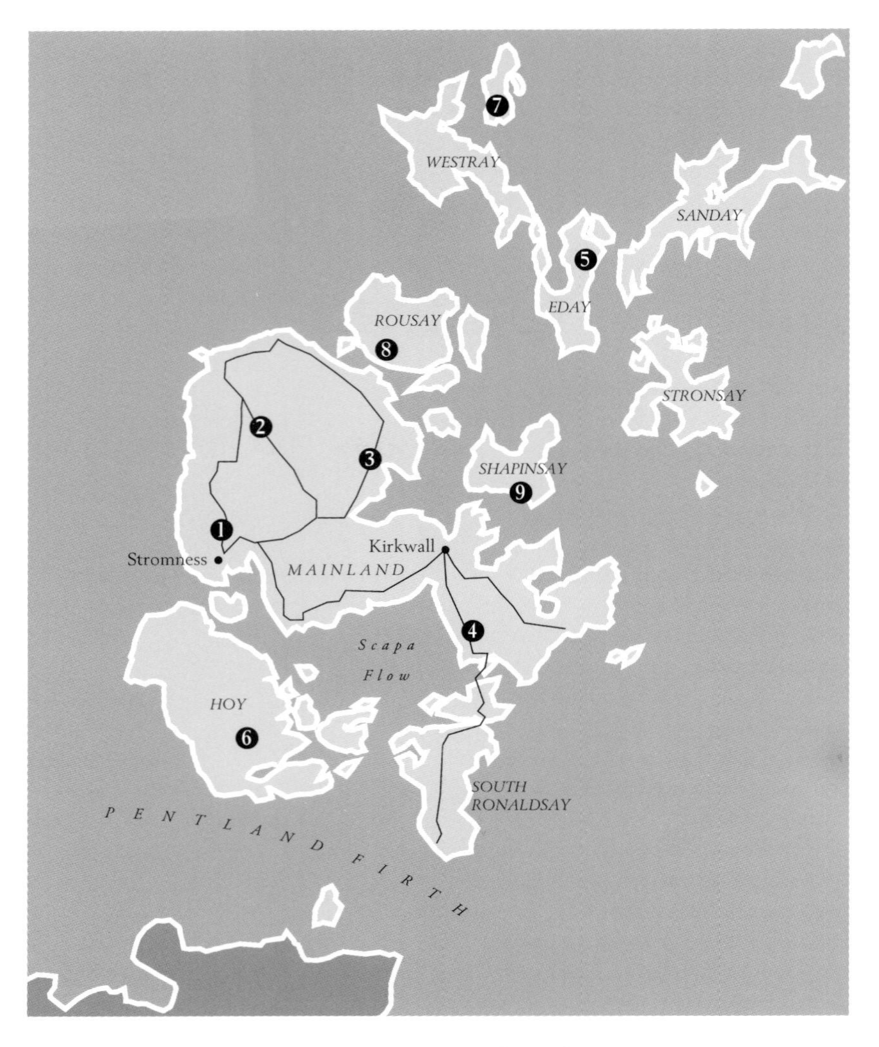

EXCURSIONS

1 Central and West Mainland

2 Stromness to Birsay

3 Kirkwall to Evie

4 Kirkwall to South Ronaldsay

5 Eday and Calf of Eday

6 Hoy

7 Papa Westray

8 Rousay

9 Shapinsay

ORKNEY

Anna Ritchie

Series Editor: Anna Ritchie

EDINBURGH: THE STATIONERY OFFICE

First published 1996

Cover photography: (Front) Stones of Stenness, (Back) Rune – inscribed armlet from the Brough of Birsay (Crown Copyright): Historic Scotland

End papers by Elisa Trimby

British Library Cataloguing in Publication Data

A catalogue record for this book is available from the British Library

Royal Commission on the Ancient and Historical Monuments of Scotland
John Sinclair House, 16 Bernard Terrace, Edinburgh EH8 9NX
0131-662 1456

The Royal Commission, which was established in 1908, is responsible for compiling a national record of archaeological sites and historic buildings of all types and periods. The Royal Commission makes this record available both through its publications (details of which can be obtained from the above address) and through the maintenance of a central archive of information, known as the National Monuments Record of Scotland. This contains the national collection of pictorial and documentary material relating to Scotland's ancient monuments and historic buildings and is open Monday to Friday for public reference at the above address.

Published by The Stationery Office and available from:
The Stationery Office Bookshops
71 Lothian Road Edinburgh EH3 9AZ
(counter service only)
South Gyle Crescent Edinburgh EH12 9EB
(mail, fax and telephone orders only)
0131-479 3141 Fax 0131-479 3142
49 High Holborn London WC1V 6HB
(counter service and fax orders only)
Fax 0171-831 1326
68-69 Bull Street Birmingham B4 6AD
0121-236 9696 Fax 0121-236 9699
33 Wine Street Bristol BS1 2BQ
0117-926 4306 Fax 0117-929 4515
9-21 Princess Street Manchester M60 8AS
0161-834 7201 Fax 0161-833 0634
16 Arthur Street Belfast BT1 4GD
01232 238451 Fax 01232 235401
The Stationery Office Oriel Bookshop
The Friary Cardiff CF1 4AA
01222 395548 Fax 01222 384347

The Stationery Office publications are also available from:
The Publications Centre
(mail, telephone and fax orders only)
PO Box 276 London SW8 5DT
General enquiries 0171-873 0011
Telephone orders 0171-873 9090
Fax orders 0171-873 8200
Accredited Agents
(see Yellow Pages)
and through good booksellers

ALSO PUBLISHED

The Highlands

Argyll and the Western Isles

Aberdeen and North-East Scotland

Glasgow, Clydeside and Stirling

Fife, Perthshire and Angus

Dumfries and Galloway

OTHER TITLES IN PREPARATION

Shetland

Edinburgh, Lothians and Borders

ISBN 0 11 495288 4

CONTENTS

FOREWORD

Twentieth-century Scotland has a heritage of human endeavour stretching back some nine thousand years, and a wide range of man-made monuments survives as proof of that endeavour. The rugged character of much of the Scottish landscape has helped to preserve many antiquities which elsewhere have vanished beneath modern development or intensive deep ploughing, though with some 10,200 km of coastline there has also been an immeasurable loss of archaeological sites as a result of marine erosion. Above all, perhaps, the preservation of such a wide range of monuments should be credited to Scotland's abundant reserves of good building stone, allowing not only the creation of extraordinarily enduring prehistoric houses and tombs but also the development of such remarkable Scottish specialities as the medieval tower-house and the iron-age broch. This volume is one of a series of nine handbooks which have been designed to provide up-to-date and authoritative introductions to the rich archaeological heritage of the various regions of Scotland, highlighting the most interesting and best preserved of the surviving monuments and setting them in their original social context. The time-scale is the widest possible, from relics of World War II or the legacy of 19th-century industrial booms back through history and prehistory to the earliest pioneer days of human settlement, but the emphasis varies from region to region, matching the particular directions in which each has developed. Some monuments are still functioning (lighthouses for instance), others are still occupied as homes, and many have been taken into the care of the State or the National Trust for Scotland, but each has been chosen as specially deserving a visit.

Thanks to the recent growth of popular interest in these topics, there is an increasing demand for knowledge to be presented in a readily digestible form and at a moderate price. In sponsoring this series, therefore, the Royal Commission on the Ancient and Historical Monuments of Scotland broadens the range of its publications with the aim of making authentic information about the man-made heritage available to as wide an audience as possible. This is the second edition of the series, in which more monuments, museums and visitor centres have been added in order to reflect the way in which the management and presentation of Scotland's past have expanded over the last decade. The excursions section proved very popular and has been both expanded and illustrated in colour.

In the first edition, Orkney and Shetland were covered in a single volume, but in this edition each of the two island groups has a volume to itself. This expanded book on Orkney reflects the rich archaeology and architecture of the islands, including the many and varied monuments from the two world wars of the 20th century. The author is a freelance archaeologist, a member of the Ancient Monuments Board for Scotland and a Trustee of the National Museums of Scotland. She has worked in Orcadian archaeology over the last thirty years. Her excavations include the neolithic settlement of

Knap of Howar and the tomb of Holm of Papa Westray North, together with a Pictish and Viking-Age farm at Buckquoy, and she was involved in devising the Pictish and Viking galleries in Tankerness House Museum.

Each major monument is numbered so that it may easily be located on the end-map, but it is recommended that the visitor should also use the relevant 1:50,000 maps published by the Ordnance Survey as its Landranger Series, particularly for the more remote sites. Sheet nos 5, 6 and 7 cover the area of this volume. The National Grid Reference is provided for each site (eg HY 488527) as well as local directions at the head of each entry.

An asterisk (*) indicates that the site is subject to restricted hours of opening; unless attributed to Historic Scotland or the National Trust for Scotland (NTS), the visitor should assume the monument to be in private ownership and **should seek permission locally to view it.** It is of course vital that visitors to any monument should observe the country code and take special care to fasten gates. Where a church is locked, it is often possible to obtain the key from the local manse, post office or general store.

We have made an attempt to estimate how accessible each monument may be for disabled visitors, indicated at the head of each entry by a wheelchair logo and a number: 1=easy access for all visitors, including those in wheelchairs; 2=reasonable access for pedestrians but restricted access for wheelchairs; 3=restricted access for all disabled but a good view from the road or parking area; 4=access for the able-bodied only.

Many of the sites mentioned in this handbook are held in trust for the nation by the Secretary of State for Scotland and cared for on his behalf by Historic Scotland. Further information about these monuments, including details of guide-books to individual properties, can be obtained from Historic Scotland, Longmore House, Salisbury Place, Edinburgh EH9 1SH. The abbreviation NMS refers to the National Museums of Scotland, Edinburgh, whose collections include important material from Orkney.

ANNA RITCHIE
Series Editor

ACKNOWLEDGEMENTS

I should like to thank Dr Graham Ritchie for his patient help and encouragement during the preparation of this volume. For their kindness in providing advice and information, I am indebted to Mrs Anne Brundle, Mr Graham Douglas, Mr John Dunbar, Ms Alison Fraser, Dr Raymond Lamb, Mr and Mrs John Rendall, Mrs Jocelyn Rendall, Mr WF Ritchie, Mr James Simpson, Mr Geoffrey Stell, Mr Bryce Wilson. The inventory and archives of the Royal Commission were an invaluable source of information, as were the lists of sites and monuments in Orkney compiled by Dr Raymond Lamb, and the work done on the chambered tombs of Orkney by Miss Audrey Henshall and Mr JH Davidson. I am very grateful for their help to the staff of the National Monuments Record and to the staff of HMSO who have worked on the production of this volume.

Most of the photographs and line drawings come from the collections of the National Monuments Record of Scotland, including photographs taken specially for this volume by Miss Marilyn Brown, Dr Graham Ritchie, Mr Steve Wallace and the author. These are all Crown Copyright: Royal Commission on the Ancient and Historical Monuments of Scotland. The maps were computer-generated by HMSO Cartographic Unit, and several site plans were drawn by Mr Ian Parker and Mr John Borland, and these are all Crown Copyright: HMSO. For the rest of the photographs and drawings, author and publisher are greatly indebted to the following individuals and institutions: Gunnie Moberg (pp.95, 125 top left); Raymond Lamb (pp.59, 67 top left, 78, 84, 100, 106, 151 bottom); Jocelyn Rendall (pp.107 top right, 108); Ian Shepherd (p.43 top); Mick Sharp (pp.33 top, 139 bottom, 148 bottom left); Mike Brooks (pp.20, 55, 56 top, 61, 69 top, 91 bottom, 92 top, 158); John Hume (p.77); Richard Welsby (p.82); J Brandon-Jones (p.65 top); Simpson and Brown Architects (p.68 top right); Neil Jackson (p.66 bottom); Professor Lord Renfrew (p.135 top left); Historic Scotland (pp.10, 11, 12, 22, 23 top, 25 bottom, 27 top, 29 top, 30, 34, 43 bottom, 44, 83, 85, 87, 88, 90 bottom, 91 top,92 bottom, 93, 94, 97, 99, 105, 109, 110, 111, 115, 118, 119, 121, 122, 124 bottom, 125 top right and bottom, 126, 127, 129, 131, 132, 133, 134, 135 top right, 139 top, 140, 144, 145, 145, 147, 150 left top and bottom, 151 top, 152, 153, 154, Crown Copyright: Historic Scotland); National Museums of Scotland (pp.14, 113 top left, 142, Copyright Trustees of the National Museums of Scotland); Scottish Record Office (p.89, Crown Copyright: HMSO); Aerofilms (p.45).

INTRODUCTION

The mound of Maes Howe in the heart of Orkney, with the Hills of Hoy beyond

The islands of Orkney have a lot to offer both visitor and resident, for there is a concentrated richness of monuments illustrating life over almost six thousand years, as well as a diverse natural heritage. Inter-island travel is easy and every island has its own special character. There are about 40 islands and as many more tiny islets and rocky skerries, but only the principal island, known as mainland, and seventeen other islands are now inhabited, some with very small populations. As elsewhere in Scotland, coastal erosion presents a serious threat to Orcadian archaeology, and, because stone has always been the primary building-material, the damage is particularly obvious as buried walls and paving become exposed in cliff-faces. There is far more visible archaeology to discover as you explore Orkney than just the monuments included in this book.

The typical Orcadian landscape is gently rounded and domestic in character, dominated by grassland. Its geological base is Old Red Sandstone, providing the flagstones that have ensured a fine tradition of drystone building since earliest times. Where these horizontal rock-beds are exposed along the shore, it is easy to appreciate what an asset they are, for the flagstone splits naturally into rectangular slabs. An experienced quarryman can produce very large and thin sheets of stone. These have been used ingeniously since prehistoric times for partition walls, byre-divisions, roofing, boxes, fences - the possibilities are endless.

The broch-settlement at Gurness shows how flagstone can be used in many ways

Most of Orkney's 956 sq km of land surface is relatively low-lying, and even the hills of Hoy, which dominate the southern skyline from much of mainland, rise no higher than 479 m above sea-level. Yet there is drama and contrast in this apparently gentle landscape. The cliffs along the Atlantic-facing west coast can rise, near-vertical, from sea-level up to 300 m, and it is an awe-inspiring experience to watch huge waves on a stormy day breaking with all the force of a turbulent ocean against Marwick Head or the great cliffs of Yesnaby. In contrast, the easterly islands of Sanday and Stronsay barely rise above the North Sea, as many an unfortunate ship's captain has discovered. Another problem for sea-travel lies in the very fact that the islands lie between the Atlantic ocean and the North Sea, for opposing currents can meet with ferocious consequences. The Pentland Firth is notoriously difficult to cross even though it is only 10 km wide, and the north-west end of tranquil Eynhallow Sound can be impassable.

The Orkney islands have been detached from the Scottish mainland since the end of the last ice age, some 10,000 years ago. Their isolation had serious repercussions for early settlers, apart from the obvious fact that they could be reached only by sea. Their fauna were very limited, for the larger mammals could not cross the Pentland Firth, and thus their native food resources were restricted to fishing and fowling. This probably explains why only a few traces have been found of the earliest human communities whose life-style depended upon hunting land mammals as well as fishing, fowling and gathering plant foods. But another factor, and one that may have obliterated traces of these people, is the continuing process of rising sea-level, for the coastline of seven thousand years ago, on which these mesolithic peoples may have camped, has vanished beneath the waves. There are sufficient clues, however, in the form of distinctive flint tools, to prove that Orkney was within the seasonal ambit of these early hunting groups.

The opening centuries of the 4th millennium BC saw an innovation in the life-style of many people across Scotland, including Orkney. This was the introduction of farming, involving a more settled way of life with cereal cultivation and the breeding of cattle, sheep and pigs, alongside new skills such as making pottery and building large and permanent structures. The latter was not difficult in Orkney with its abundant good stone, and there was plenty of clay available for the potter's craft, but the essential ingredients for farming all had to be imported. Young animals and seed corn had to be transported across the Pentland Firth, probably in hide-covered boats. Dogs were needed too, and deer appear to have been introduced deliberately, though they would roam freely once established.

Coastal erosion reveals walling near Skara Brae

These farming pioneers benefited from a climate that was slightly warmer than today, allowing not only barley but the less hardy wheat to be grown. Analysis of pollen and other plant remains has shown that initially the Orcadian landscape included light woodland, mainly of birch and alder, but that by around 3000 BC the woodland had been largely replaced by open grassland and heath, the virtually treeless environment of today. The cause was a combination of several factors, including the farmers' own efforts in clearing woodland for arable fields and fuel. But there seems also to have been an increase in wind-speed, which led to plant-damage, coastal erosion and the accelerated formation of sand-dunes. This was linked to an overall and gradual deterioration in climate, which has continued with good patches and bad patches to the present day. It was a prolonged bad patch that led to the formation of blanket peat over parts of Orkney, as elsewhere in Scotland, towards the end of the 2nd millennium BC. Peat was to become an essential source of fuel but it obliterated large areas of formerly productive agricultural land.

The success of the early colonization of Orkney may be gauged from the remarkable ceremonial and funerary monuments that survive alongside the domestic settlements. The communities capable of sparing the labour and of organizing the labour to build such colossal public monuments as the Ring of Brodgar (no. 64) were living at an average standard far beyond that of mere subsistence. The earliest monuments are tombs, reflecting not only the importance of ancestors but also their origins. Comparison of the design of tombs and of the objects found in them indicates that the Orkney islands were settled by people who had previously lived in Caithness. There is no evidence of colonization across the North Sea from Scandinavia, an orientation that was to become paramount in Viking times; throughout prehistory, the islands looked southwards into the rest of the British Isles for new ideas and influences. Nor is there evidence of any major influx of new blood between the original colonization and the Viking settlement of the 9th century AD, although it is unlikely that the population remained entirely static.

Despite their location in the far north of Britain, the Orkney islands participated in the same overall technological and ideological development as the rest of the country, but the level of participation varied. During the first half of the 3rd millennium, a traveller from southern England would have found much that was familiar in Orkney, from ceremonial monuments to pottery styles, but by 2000 BC the islands seem to have become culturally insular. It may be that the first thousand or so years of farming were too successful, in the sense that the land became impoverished and the standard of living dropped. New fashions in pottery and the magical new technology of bronze-working barely touched Orcadian life, although burial customs changed in line with communities farther south. The old tombs that could hold bones of tens or even hundreds of people were replaced by individual burials, often cremated, in stone cists or pits, covered by earthen mounds. But there were flashes of the old brilliance. One burial at the Knowes of Trotty (no. 69) was accompanied by gold and amber gravegoods fit for a powerful chieftain.

Orkney was certainly not immune to the general increase in competition for resources and social aggression of the first millennium BC. This is reflected in the architectural record by the stone-built forts known as brochs, which came to dominate the landscape of the last few centuries BC and the first two centuries AD. Brochs were built throughout northern Scotland and the Western Isles, and several survive higher than those in Orkney, but nowhere else can you appreciate the internal fittings and external domestic settlements better than at Gurness (no. 53) and Midhowe (no. 55). The Roman fleet must have passed many a broch on its way round the north of Scotland, sent by Agricola in AD 83 to check that Britain was indeed an island and to warn its inhabitants of the might of Rome. But that was the closest encounter that Orkney had with the Roman military machine.

The two most important legacies of the Roman presence in Scotland involved politics and religion. Military campaigns north of the Firth of Forth had the effect of unifying the Celtic tribes into larger and thereby stronger political units, a process which led by the 6th century to the emergence of the kingdom of the Picts. The Roman occupation of northern England brought Christianity in its wake, and this new religion gradually replaced the old Celtic gods in southern Scotland in the 5th and 6th centuries, and in Pictland in the 6th and 7th centuries.

This fashionable cape with its long fringe was found in a peat bog in Orkney and dates to Pictish times.

Combining archaeological evidence with the few historical references to Orkney, there is no doubt that the islands were part of Pictland, but it is difficult to judge their political status within that kingdom. Orkney had its own ruler, who appears to have owed allegiance to the Pictish high-king, but on occasion there were Orcadian hostages at the Pictish court, presumably to ensure good behaviour in the islands, and punitive expeditions were sometimes dispatched to the far north of the kingdom.

Christianity was brought to Orkney first by Irish missionary monks in the late 6th and 7th centuries, and by the 8th century there were strong ties between the Church in Orkney and that in eastern Pictland and Northumbria. These links are most clearly seen in stone sculpture. The Pictish symbol stone from the Knowe of Burrian in mainland Orkney is astoundingly close in the design of its eagle to the evangelist symbol of the eagle of St John in the illustrated gospel-book known as the Book of Kells, created mostly at Iona in the 8th century (the stone is in Tankerness House Museum and the Book in Trinity College Library, Dublin). The front panel of a stone altar from Flotta suggests that there was an important church there around AD 800, for the panel is carved with a cross infilled with finely executed interlace decoration.

All these links were disrupted, however, towards the end of the 8th century, when the islands found themselves centre-stage in the vibrant new world of the Viking Age. Shiploads of Viking warriors from the fjords of western Norway raided the Northern Isles on their way to plunder the rich monasteries of western Scotland and Ireland. Shetland was geographically closer to Norway but it was the fertile grasslands of Orkney that attracted the most intensive settlement by Norwegian families in the course of the 9th century, leading to the creation of a powerful Norse earldom based in Orkney and controlling Shetland and Caithness.

The discovery of Norse farms and pagan graves testifies to the economic success of the earldom, but the most dramatic proof lies in the density of Scandinavian placenames, all but obliterating earlier indigenous names. They are a superb source of information in themselves. They identify the areas of Norway from which the settlers came, because there was a natural tendency to bestow upon the new lands the familiar placenames of the homeland, particularly those relating to topography. Thus Sandwick meaning sand bay, or Minna Geo meaning narrow inlet are purely descriptive names, while Skippie Geo means ships' inlet and indicates a natural landing-place, and Lyber Ness means lythe-rock-ness and refers to a rock at the end of a headland (ness) from which lythes (fish now known as pollacks) could be caught. Some names incorporate personal names, such as Glims Holm which means Glum's islet after the Old Norse name *Glumr*, and Sweyn Holm or Svein's islet. Many farm-names contain the basic generic terms *stathr*, dwelling-place or farm, *bolstathr*, farm, and *setr*, dwelling, as in Ocklster, Kirbuster and Mossetter, indicating the type of settlement. High-status estates can be identified in placenames using the element *boer*, as in Trenaby, and *bu*, as in the Bu of Rapness.

The enduring blanket effect of Scandinavian placenames was such that it left little opportunity for later Scottish naming in the Northern Isles. The modern Orcadian dialect contains many Scots words, in some cases fossilized 16th-century words adopted during a period of maximum immigration from lowland Scotland, and in other cases farming terms reflecting the influx in the 19th century of farmers from north-east Scotland. But placenames have remained essentially Scandinavian, even where they can be shown to be of relatively recent coining.

Names derived from the Old Norse *borg*, meaning fort, can be very confusing in the context of Orcadian archaeology. The term occurs as broch and as brough, both of which are pronounced in the same way, but, while a broch is indeed a stone fort, a brough is a steep promontory almost or entirely detached from the mainland and thus naturally defensive, such as the Brough of Birsay and the Brough of Deerness.

St Magnus Cathedral and the ruined Earl's Palace in the 18th century

A group of placenames of special interest in connection with the early Christian Church is that containing the element *papar*. It is clear from early Norse documentary sources that papar was the name given to Irish hermits in Iceland, and there are *papar* placenames in Iceland as there are in the Northern Isles and Caithness. Such names were often associated with small islands or remote coastal areas, the locations favoured by ascetic hermits looking for 'a desert place in the ocean', but in Orkney and Shetland papa names are associated with fertile islands of some size and importance. Orcadian examples include the islands of Papa Westray and Papa Stronsay, the first probably the seat of a 9th-century bishopric and the second the island to which the Norse earls sent for malt for their Christmas ale. This suggests that the Scandinavian *papar*-names here reflect Norse acceptance of important ecclesiastical centres, themselves founded on the sound economics of prime farmland.

Intermarriage and the use of Pictish slaves in Norse households ensured that Christianity was adopted by the Norse settlers in the course of the later 9th and 10th centuries. Although the official conversion of the earldom took place in 995, as a result of a visit by the Norwegian king, Olaf Tryggvason, linguistic and archaeological evidence combine to suggest that the process of conversion was underway earlier. There are early placenames incorporating the Norse element *kirkja*, meaning church, such as Kirbister, and pagan Viking graves give way to Christian burials from the mid 10th century.

With the establishment of the great Norse earldom of the north, the Northern Isles enter the realm of history proper. The fortunes of the earls and other leading families are recorded in several Icelandic sagas but especially in *Orkneyinga Saga*, compiled around AD 1200. The story makes fascinating reading even today. Its author was clearly more familiar with Orkney and Caithness than with Shetland, but that is a reflection of the power bias of the earldom, in which the most important families had estates in Orkney and Caithness. The saga is primarily concerned with events of the 11th and 12th centuries, which was a golden age in Orkney, beginning with the exploits of Earl Thorfinn and encompassing the life and martyrdom of Earl Magnus, for whom the great cathedral was built in Kirkwall, initially by Earl Rognvald.

The bishopric of Orkney and Shetland was founded in the 11th century, and the bishop's seat was recorded at Birsay around 1160. Once the building of St Magnus Cathedral was underway, the bishops resided there and the episcopal complex at Birsay was abandoned. Initially the bishopric was associated with the archbishoprics of Hamburg-Bremen and York, but from 1154 it was transferred to the new province of Nidaros (Trondheim). Even after the earldom of Orkney and Shetland was split in 1194, the islands remained in the same bishopric, its clergy mostly Norwegian until the later 15th century when Scots became increasingly predominant. In 1472 the bishopric was transferred to the see of St Andrews. The ancient connection with Nidaros was commemorated in 1937 by a gift from the Church of Norway to St Magnus Cathedral of a replica of the statue of St Olaf at Nidaros Cathedral.

Once Christianity had been accepted by leading Norsemen, many small chapels were built in the 12th century to serve family estates and several of these survive today. It is usually, but not always, the chapels which did not become parish churches that remain, ruinous but little altered, whereas parish churches underwent sometimes drastic rebuilding. Considerable stimulus to this 12th-century building programme must have been provided by the immense project going on in Kirkwall with the creation of St Magnus Cathedral, which began in 1137. As the relics of St Magnus were to be housed in this new cathedral, perhaps it was local pride that prompted the building of a new church in Egilsay where the saint had been murdered.

As a result of its involvement in Norwegian civil wars, the earldom was split in 1194, with Shetland placed under the direct control of Norway and half of Orkney's revenue assigned to the Norwegian Crown. After the death of Earl John in 1231, Caithness passed to the Scottish Crown, and thereafter all the Orkney earls were of Scottish blood, even though they owed allegiance to Norway. Finally, both Orkney (1468) and Shetland (1469) were pledged to Scotland as part of the complex negotiations attending the marriage of Margaret, daughter of King Christian I of Denmark and Norway, with James III of Scotland.

Dundas Street, Stromness, photographed by Erskine Beveridge in 1894

Apart from St Magnus Cathedral and the unique round church at Orphir, the medieval churches of Orkney were simple unpretentious structures which did not incur the wrath of the 1560 Scottish Reformation. Nor were there rich monasteries to punish, although it may not be a coincidence that the small monastery on Eynhallow appears to have been secularized in the 16th century. Even St Magnus Cathedral survived the Reformation unscathed, though it had a narrow escape at the hands of the Earl of Caithness in 1614 during the insurrection of Robert Stewart.

The later 15th and 16th centuries witnessed frequent power-struggles between the ruling families of the Northern Isles and the Scottish Crown, and the political turbulence of the period is reflected in its buildings. The development of Kirkwall was closely linked with royal efforts to curb the power of the Sinclairs in the late 15th century, for the town was made a royal burgh in 1486, and it was given possession of the cathedral as a counter-measure against the Sinclairs' advantage in owning the castle in Kirkwall, the cathedral being the only large defensible building on a comparable scale to the castle. The cathedral belongs to the people of Kirkwall to this day, but the castle was demolished long ago.

The Stewart earls were particularly ruthless and ambitious, and the years of their rule from 1567 to 1615 were grimly oppressive, but they have bequeathed a fine heritage in Earl Robert's palace at Birsay and Earl Patrick's palace at Kirkwall. Smaller fortified houses were built by leading families during the 17th century, and these have endured rebuildings to the present day, but nothing survives of the contemporary homes of peasant farmers and fishermen. Despite an often archaic appearance, most of the extant farm steadings are no older than the 19th century, but the traditions of construction and the way of life that they represent is much older. The importance of this vernacular architecture has been recognized with the establishment of the two farm museums at Corrigall and Kirbuster.

Kirkwall developed as a trading centre and as an administrative centre for both Church and secular state from the 12th century, whereas Stromness and St Margaret's Hope are relative latecomers and owe their existence to the expansion of trade and fishing in the 18th and 19th centuries. Orkney's location between the Atlantic Ocean and the North Sea also ensured a focal naval role in the wars of the 19th and 20th centuries. Like the herring fishing boom, wartime brought a temporary influx of vast numbers of people. The impact on Orcadian economy of the Second World War has been described as 'some monstrous tourist bonanza', for it created a captive market of thousands of servicemen and women. The ruins of many military and naval installations may still be seen, and it is not difficult to appreciate the wartime importance of Scapa Flow when visiting gun batteries such as those on Hoxa Head, or the naval base at Lyness.

Until as recently as 300 years ago, there were no marine charts to guide shipping round the hazardous coasts of the Northern Isles, and navigation relied upon personal experience and knowledge of coastal waters. The Pentland Firth is particularly dangerous. In the days of sailing ships, it was known as 'hell's mouth' because of its ferocious eddies and tidal races, and many ships preferred the longer route round the north of Orkney. With the growth of the fishing industry in the 17th and 18th centuries, the need for lighthouses became imperative, and the first lights provided in the Northern Isles were those on North Ronaldsay and the Pentland Skerries, built at the end of the 18th century, and on Sanday in the early 19th century.

Throughout the 19th century, the Northern Lighthouse Board was served by outstanding engineers from the Stevenson family, and it was in the company of Robert Stevenson and the Commissioners of the Northern

World War II gun batteries on Hoxa Head

Lights that Sir Walter Scott made his famous voyage around Scotland in 1814. In the journal that he kept, Sir Walter describes a visit to see the lighthouse on Sanday, where he was struck by the high standard of the keepers' living quarters: 'All in excellent order and the establishment of the keepers in the same style of comfort and respectability as elsewhere - far better than the house of the master of Fair Isle and rivalling my own baronial mansion of Abbotsford'. One is left wondering if he really approved of such comforts!

Visiting archaeological sites often takes you into areas of outstanding natural interest. As you explore the shoreline, you may well find yourself under scrutiny from seals swimming offshore. Both grey and common seals are frequent, and there is the chance of seeing porpoises, dolphins and whales. Coastal plant-life is varied and colourful, with drifts of pink thrift and, if you are lucky, the purple flowers of the tiny Scottish primrose. The Royal Society for the Protection of Birds has a number of reserves in Orkney, many of them as remarkable for their plant cover as for the birds. The reserves range from seabird colonies such as those on Marwick Head on the west coast of mainland, the Noup Cliffs of Westray and North Hill in Papa Westray, with their guillemots and kittiwakes, to wetland sites such as Mill Dam in Shapinsay with its breeding ducks and pintails and, in winter, its visiting whooper swans and greylag geese. A small reserve in Egilsay protects the elusive corncrake, while a huge area of northern Hoy encompasses a wide range of birds including great skuas, puffins, Manx shearwaters and a number of moorland species, as well as mountain hares.

The history and development of the Orkney islands over the last five and a half thousand years are well illustrated by a wide range of stone buildings and earthworks. Some conform to fashions widespread beyond the islands, demonstrating that their peripheral geographical location was rarely matched by any cultural isolation, while others have a special interest as examples of responses to local conditions of climate or resources.

EXCURSIONS

These are day-long excursions, chosen for the wide variety of monuments that they encompass; some involve using a car and others are best followed on foot (indicated on the maps as a broken line). Encouraged by Orkney Islands Council, many local community councils have produced useful leaflet guides to the natural and built environments of their individual areas or islands.

KEY

- Bridge
- Broch, fort
- Cairn
- Castle
- Church
- Harbour
- House, rural building
- Industrial Monument
- Lighthouse
- Military Monument
- Miscellaneous prehistoric
- Monument
- Pictish Stone
- Standing Stone
- Stone Circle
- Town, village
- Town *explored in text*
- Henge
- Round Cairn
- Viking Settlement V

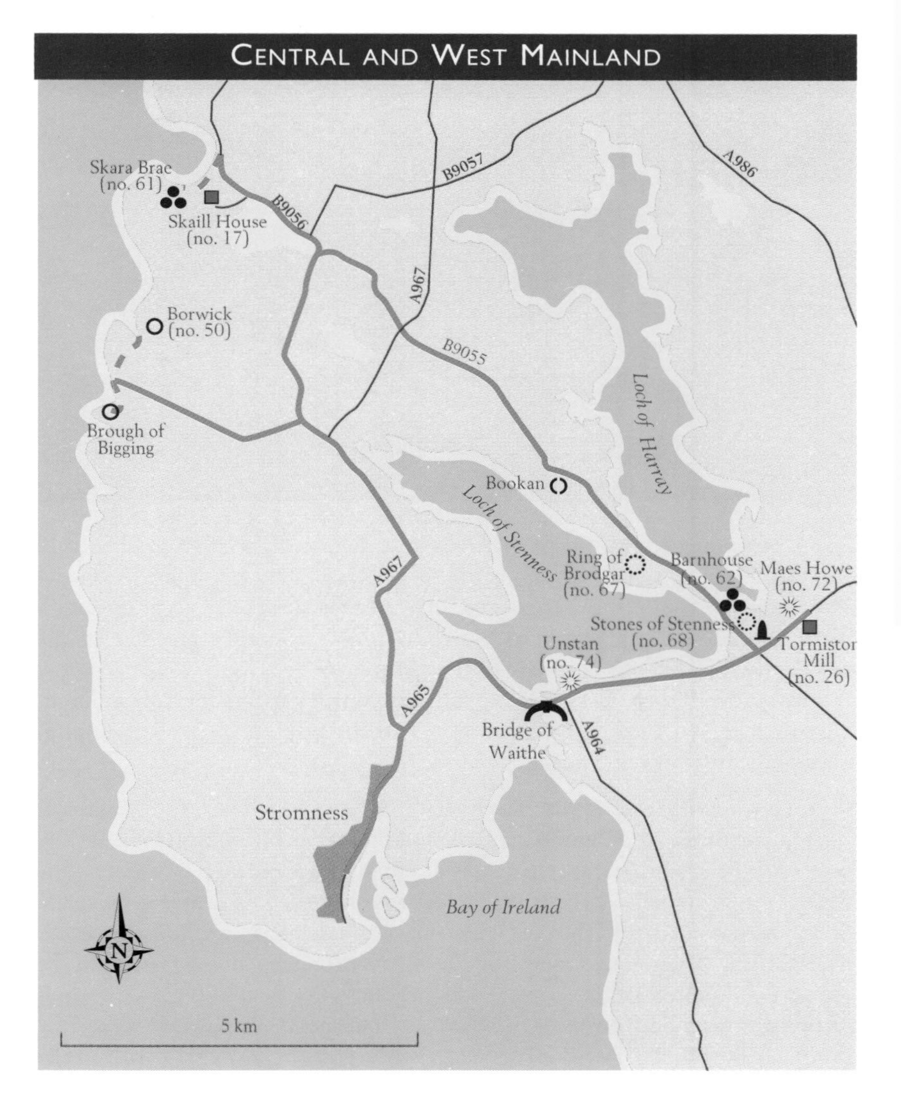

Reconstructed foundations of neolithic houses at Barnhouse

From Stromness, take the A 965 towards Kirkwall; as the road swings eastwards along the south shore of the Loch of Stenness, the Bridge of Waithe spans the outflow from the loch into the sea, a stone bridge with three segmental arches built in 1859 to replace an earlier wooden bridge that consisted of logs laid across low stone piers (HY 281112). Almost immediately after the bridge is the signposted track to the fort and tomb at Unstan (no. 74). Continue on the A 965 to the mill at Tormiston (no. 26) and the great tomb of Maes Howe (no. 72).

Retrace your route along the main road, noting in a field on the right the Barnhouse Stone, a magnificent slab standing over 3 m high (HY 312121), over which the sun sets at midwinter and shines down the passage into the Maes Howe tomb. Take the B 9055 northwards to the henge and stone circle at Stenness (no. 65) and the contemporary settlement at Barnhouse (no. 62). The Stones of Stenness and the Ring of Brodgar (no. 64) should be appreciated together as a great ceremonial complex, along with their outlying stones and burial mounds. Continue north-westwards along the B 9055, past the Ring of Bookan just visible as a circular earthwork in the field to the left (HY 283144), an unusual monument which may be a small henge. At the Loch of Skaill, the road joins the B 9056 and skirts the north-east side of the loch to the carpark for Skara Brae on the Bay of Skaill (no. 61). Set back from the bay is the imposing 17th-century Skaill House (no. 17).

From Skaill, follow the B 9056 south to the signposted turning for Yesnaby, an area of great natural beauty and considerable interest for geologists and botanists. The cliffs rise to a sheer height of some 30 m OD, and exposure to sea-spray has created a special environment for plants, suppressing the heather and encouraging plants such as crowberry, wild squill, sea pinks and wild thyme. A walk along the cliffs to the north allows a visit to the broch of Borwick (no. 50), while to the south there is a promontory fort, the Brough of Bigging (HY 218157), marked by two ramparts, about 30 m apart, across the neck of the promontory.

A pastoral scene at sunlit Stones of Stenness

The broch of Borwick stands proud on the Atlantic coast of mainland Orkney

Stromness to Birsay

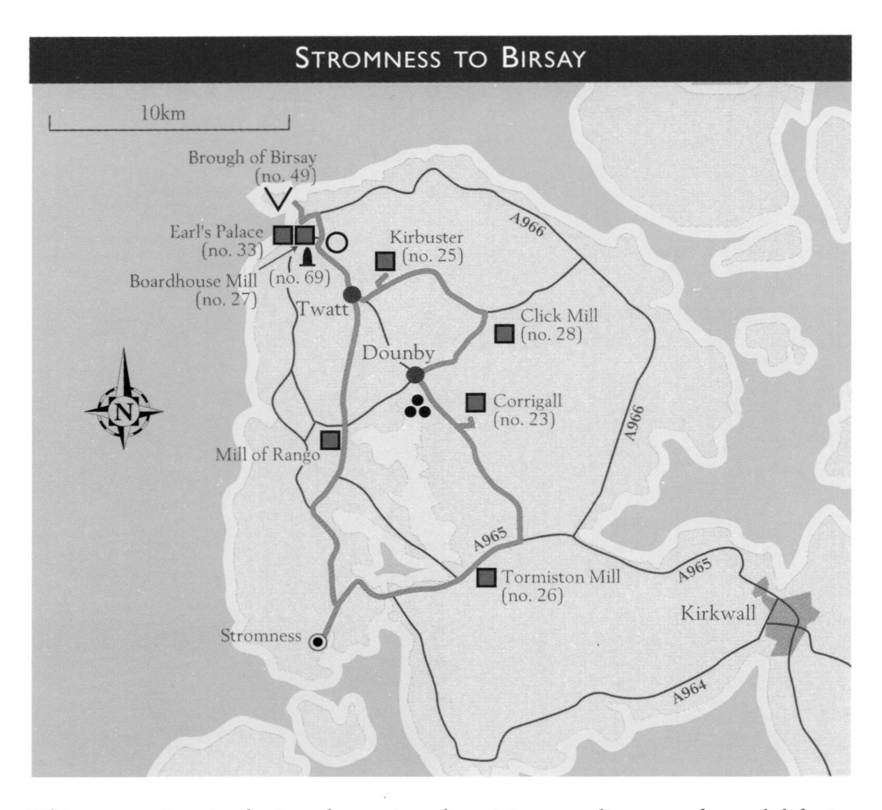

This excursion is designed to give the visitor a glimpse of rural life in Orkney in recent centuries. From Stromness, take the A 965 eastwards, past Tormiston Mill (no. 26), and turn left on to the A 986. After about 5 km, the farm museum at Corrigall is signposted on the right (no. 23). Continue on the A 986 to Dounby, passing in a field on the left before reaching Dounby a large burnt mound known as Fan Knowe (HY 299197). At the crossroads in Dounby turn right on the B 9057 to visit the click mill (no. 28). About 0.5 km farther on, turn left on to a minor road; after 5 km, turn right for the Kirbuster farm museum (no. 25) with its sheltered garden.

One of Orkney's most attractive mills at Tormiston

Farm buildings at Kirbuster

Return south along the minor road to rejoin the A 986 at Twatt, turning right and joining the A 967 along the side of the Loch of Boardhouse. The tall Stane o'Quoybune is in a field on the left (no. 66) and on the right, near the junction of the A 967 and B 9056, is a low stony mound, the remains of Oxtro broch (HY 254267). From the head of the loch, the Barony burn runs into Birsay Bay, powering the Boardhouse mills on the way (no. 27). About 0.5 km beyond Boardhouse, turn left on to the A 966 for Birsay village and the imposing Earl's Palace (no. 33). The simple parish church of 1760 incorporates a 17th-century belfry and a 13th-century lancet window from earlier churches on the same spot (no. 38). The old manse was built in 1761 and from 1774 it was the home of the Reverend George Low, who recorded many of the antiquities of the Northern Isles.

Inside the house at Kirbuster

Follow the signposted track round the north side of the bay and, if the tide is low, visit the Pictish and Viking settlement and church on the Brough of Birsay (no. 49). Return to Stromness via the A 967, passing the restored 19th-century Mill of Rango beside the Loch of Harray (HY 265181).

The Brough of Birsay is isolated at high tide

KIRKWALL TO EVIE

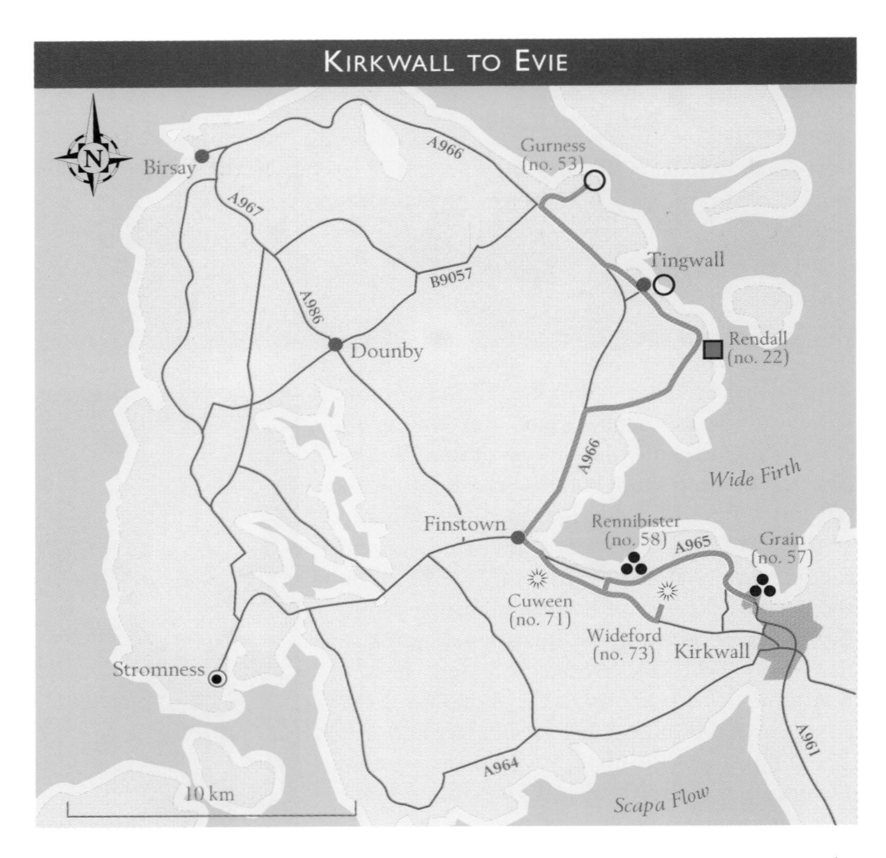

Leave Kirkwall on the A 965, pausing on the outskirts to visit Grain earth-house (no. 57) signposted on the right in the industrial estate. After some 6km another earth-house may be visited at Rennibister (no. 58). Just over 1km beyond Rennibister, turn left and follow the signs for the chambered tomb perched on the side of Wideford Hill (no. 73). Return along the minor road to the signposted chambered tomb of Cuween (no. 71).

Across the Bay of Finstown rises Wideford Hill

Continue into Finstown and turn right on the A 966. After about 5 km, take the signposted right turn for the 17th-century Hall of Rendall dovecote (no. 22). Continue north along this minor road to Tingwall, the site of Orkney's Viking-Age parliament; the great mound covers the remains of an iron-age broch (HY 401229) but it may also have been the focus point for the assembled Norsemen. Rejoin the A 966 and continue to Evie to visit the broch of Gurness with its remarkable stone-built village (no. 53).

A rare example of a beehive-shaped dovecote at Hall of Rendall

The broch at Gurness was ideally placed to monitor activities in Eynhallow Sound

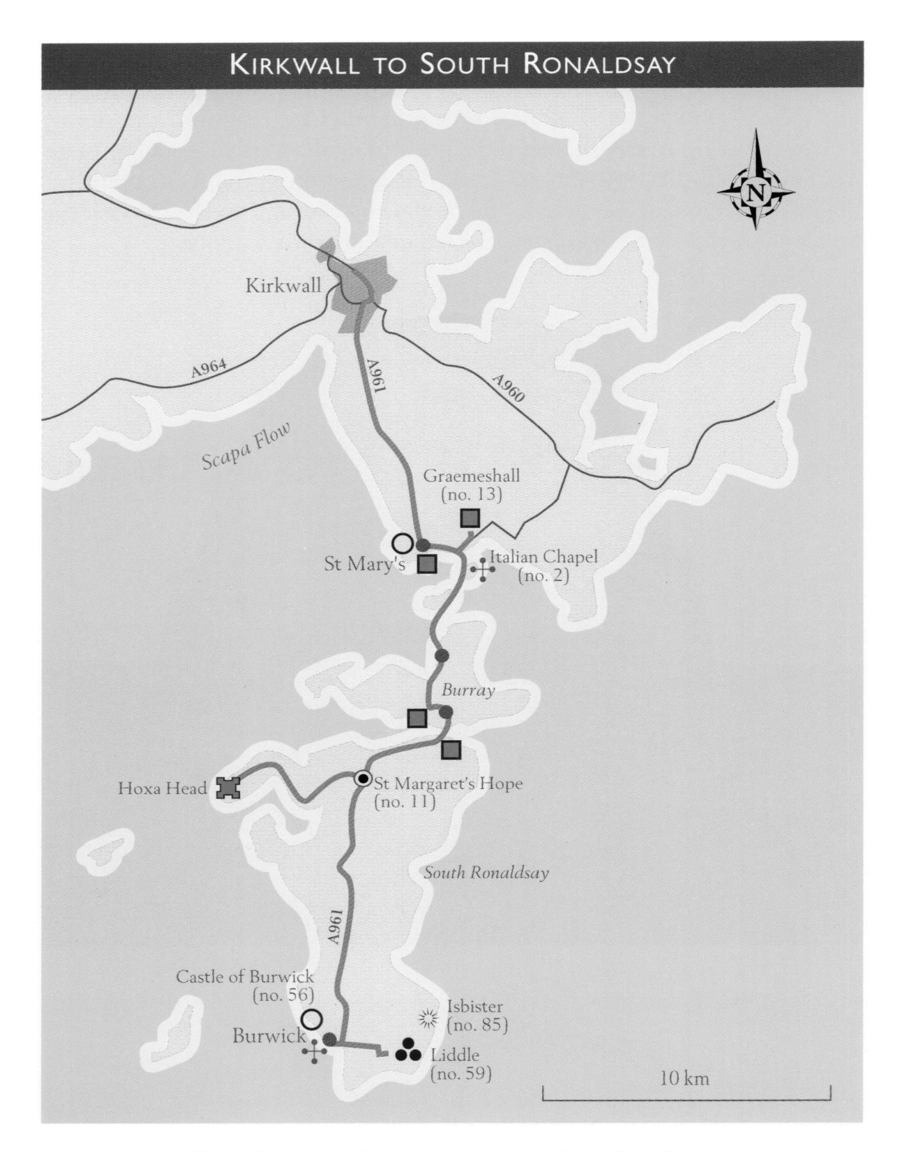

Leave Kirkwall on the A 961 for St Mary's. On the right of the road entering the village is a large mound beside the Loch of Ayre; this is the remains of an extensive broch-complex. St Mary's was a thriving fishing village until the first of the Churchill Barriers cut off access to the open sea. Near the shore is a large grain storehouse with crowstepped gables and forestair, which was built in 1608 to serve the Meal estate. The house of Meal was the precursor of Graemeshall (no. 13), some 1.5 km east of St Mary's on the B 9052.

Return from Graemeshall to the A 961 and cross the Churchill Barriers (no. 1) first to Lamb Holm and the Italian Chapel (no. 2), and thence to Glimps Holm and Burray; if the tide is low, look for the blockships sunk during the First World War to prevent German submarines from slipping between the islands into the Scapa Flow anchorage. The small and fertile island of Burray has been a favoured place for settlement since prehistoric

The Italian Chapel is a potent reminder of the Second World War

St Margaret's Hope, once a flourishing North Sea port

A gun emplacement in the Balfour Battery gave a wide view over Scapa Flow from Hoxa Head

times, and some unusual and prestigious artefacts have come from a broch at the north end, including an egg carved of serpentine and decorated bone mounts (in Tankerness House Museum). The beautiful crescentic bay on the east side of the island attracted Viking-Age settlement, reflected in the place-name Bu, an Old Norse word meaning 'feasting hall', and a large hoard of Viking silver was found in a bog on the island in 1889. The house now known as the Bu of Burray dates from the 18th century, and in the harbour in Burray village is a grain storehouse built in 1645 for an earlier owner of the estate.

Cross from Burray to South Ronaldsay on the fourth of the Churchill Barriers, and visit the Fossil Museum. Continue on the A 961 and take the B 9043 into St Margaret's Hope (no. 11). Follow the B 9063 to Hoxa and a minor road out to the 20th-century gun batteries on Hoxa Head (no. 3).

Return to St Margaret's Hope and continue south on the A 961 to Burwick. In the bleak St Mary's Church (1789 with an interior redesigned in 1898) is a large flat boulder carved with a pair of footprints (p.125). From here it is possible to walk to the iron-age Castle of Burwick (no. 56). From the bend just before the A 961 terminates at Burwick, follow the B 9041 and the signposts to Liddle burnt mound (no. 59) and Isbister chambered tomb (no. 85).

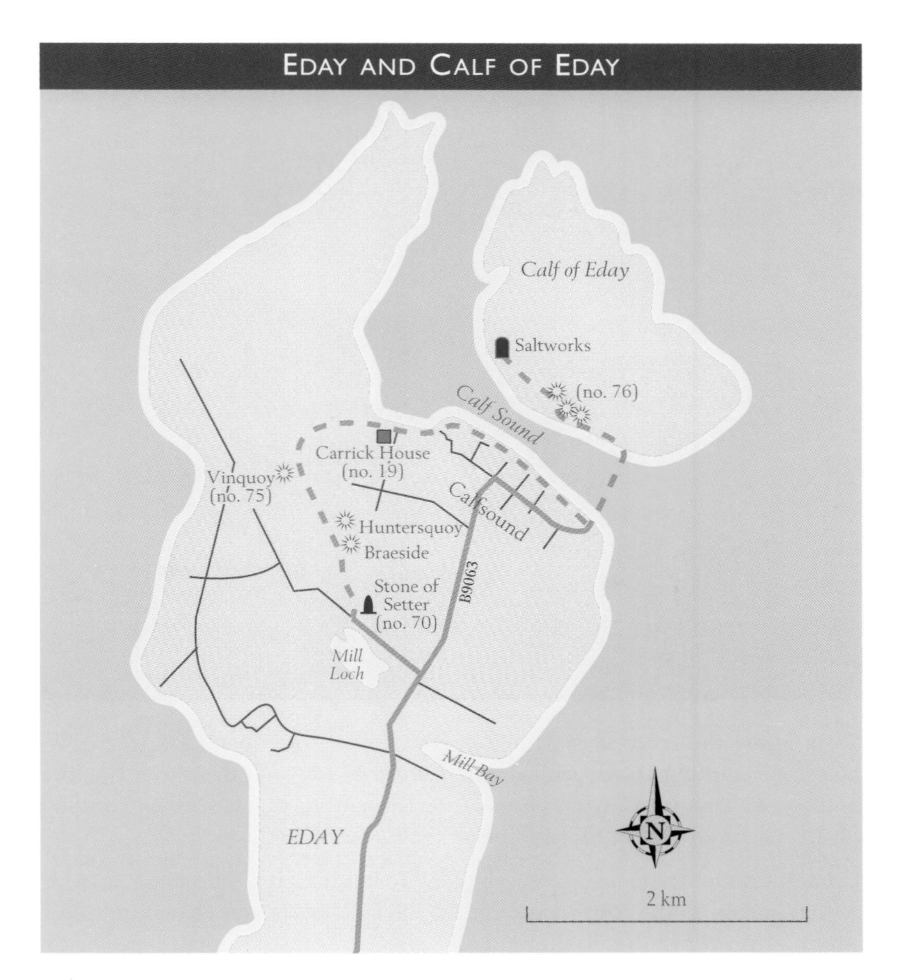

The northern part of Eday, and the adjacent small island, Calf of Eday, are particularly interesting for their prehistoric archaeology; in contrast to the peat-covered landscape of today, Eday was in early prehistoric times a fertile and densely settled area, as the discovery of ancient field-boundaries beneath the blanket of peat has demonstrated. The visitor arriving by sea at Backaland or by air at London should take a taxi (via the Eday co-operative to arrange a boat for the Calf) to just beyond Mill Loch (a Site of Special Scientific Interest on account of its breeding colony of Red-throated Divers) and begin this walking tour with the Stone of Setter (no. 70). This is one of the tallest single standing stones in the Northern Isles, and the effect of natural weathering has sculpted the sandstone into a distinctively furrowed profile. Its location was specifically designed to dominate the valleys to north and south, that to the north containing a number of chambered tombs and burial mounds, and a remarkable, but undatable, stone enclosure. Walking north-westwards, much of the stonework of the chamber of Braeside tomb is visible (HY 563375), but little more than the entrance passage to the lower chamber may be seen of the two-storey tomb of Huntersquoy (HY 562377). High above, on Vinquoy Hill (no. 75), is a well-preserved chambered tomb with superb views over the neighbouring islands.

The red sandstone of Eday was used in St Magnus Cathedral

Walk along the crest of the ridge northwards to the opening in the dyke before attempting to descend north-eastwards towards the shore of Calf Sound; skirt round Carrick House (no. 19), a 17th-century house famous for its association with the capture of the pirate, John Gow, in 1725.

Continue south-eastwards along the road towards Calf Sound pier, and hire a boat across to the south-west end of the Calf. This is a charming small island, now uninhabited, and a pleasant walk north-westwards encompasses not only well-preserved chambered tombs and the remains of an iron-age settlement but also a most unusual monument of industrial archaeology. Two of the tombs have small subterranean chambers and passages, dug into the hillside (HY 578386), which, though overgrown, may still be entered. Their oval chambers are divided by radial slabs into small burial compartments, and they appear originally to have been covered by low round cairns. A short distance further on along the coast is a larger composite tomb, which was entirely uncovered by excavation and left open so that the structure is quite clear (no. 76).

Follow the shore northwards to see the ruins of a 17th-century saltworks, an unusual industrial legacy and unique in the Northern Isles (HY 574391 and HY 575387). Both buildings were originally rectangular and lie end-on to the sea: the seaward gable was curved and stood in the sea, while the inland gable was cut into the slope of the land. A very thick wall divided the building into two, with a large fireplace on either side to evaporate the salt-water and dry the salt - the fireplace surviving in the south building has a rounded arch.

Braeside chambered tomb lies open to the skies

Carrick House overlooks Papa Sound

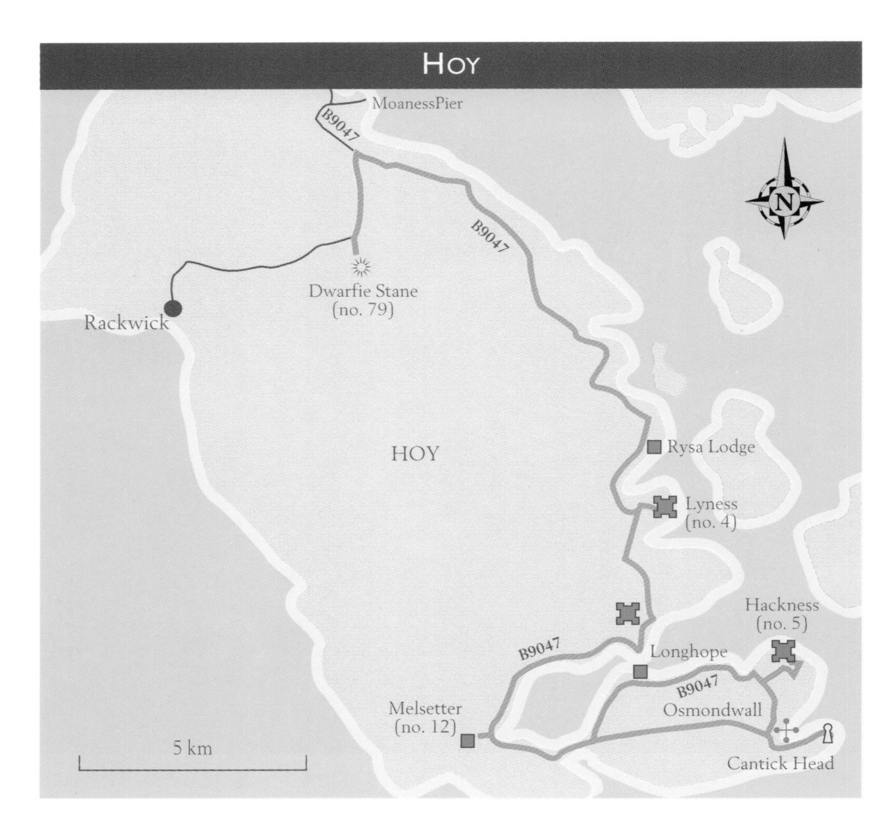

The route suggested here assumes that the visitor has arrived at Lyness by the car ferry from Houton, but it could easily be followed in reverse by visitors arriving at Moaness by passenger ferry from Stromness, if a hired car is booked in advance. At Lyness, explore the remains of the naval base used in two World Wars, especially the Scapa Flow Visitor Centre in the old pumping station (no. 4). Take the B 9047 southwards, passing the striking black and white art deco building at ND 307923; this was the frontage of a cinema and theatre built during the Second World War to entertain the large garrison.

The ultimate in early 19th-century coastal security, a martello tower at Hackness

Art Deco comes to Orkney: a cinema for the Lyness garrison

Lethaby's transformation of Melsetter House

Continue on the B 9047 to Longhope to see the old Custom House built in the early 19th century when this was an important anchorage. The main entrance is graced by pillars and two lions above. Follow the road eastwards along the coast to visit the martello tower and battery at Hackness (no.5) and south to Osmondwall. In the churchyard is a 17th-century burial-aisle belonging to the Moodie family of Melsetter; it is a small rectangular building with crowstepped gables and a flagged roof, and the round arch of the door is embellished with an inscribed moulding. The former church was dedicated to St Colm, and an Early Christian cross-slab was found in its foundations when it was demolished (NMS). The road continues round the bay of Kirk Hope to the lighthouse on Cantick Head (HY 346894), which was built in 1858 by David and Thomas Stevenson.

Return along the minor road from Osmondwall to the B 9047 south of Longhope, and continue west to the beautiful house of Melsetter (no.12), the oldest part of which was built in 1738 but which is famous for its enhancement in 1898 by WR Lethaby. In 1904, Lethaby designed a hunting lodge for Melsetter, again based on an existing building, a small cottage that became the servants' quarters of the new Rysa Lodge. This can be seen on the right of the B 9047 some 10 km north-east of Melsetter at HY 305962.

Continue on the B 9047 to the crossroads south of Moaness and turn left along a minor road signposted to Rackwick. After 2 km there is a carpark for visitors to the Dwarfie Stane (no. 79). This extraordinary rock-cut tomb lies on the hillside commanding the valley between Rackwick Bay to the south and Bay of Quoys to the north.

The rock-cut tomb known as the Dwarfie Stane was a remarkable achievement for Hoy's neolithic inhabitants

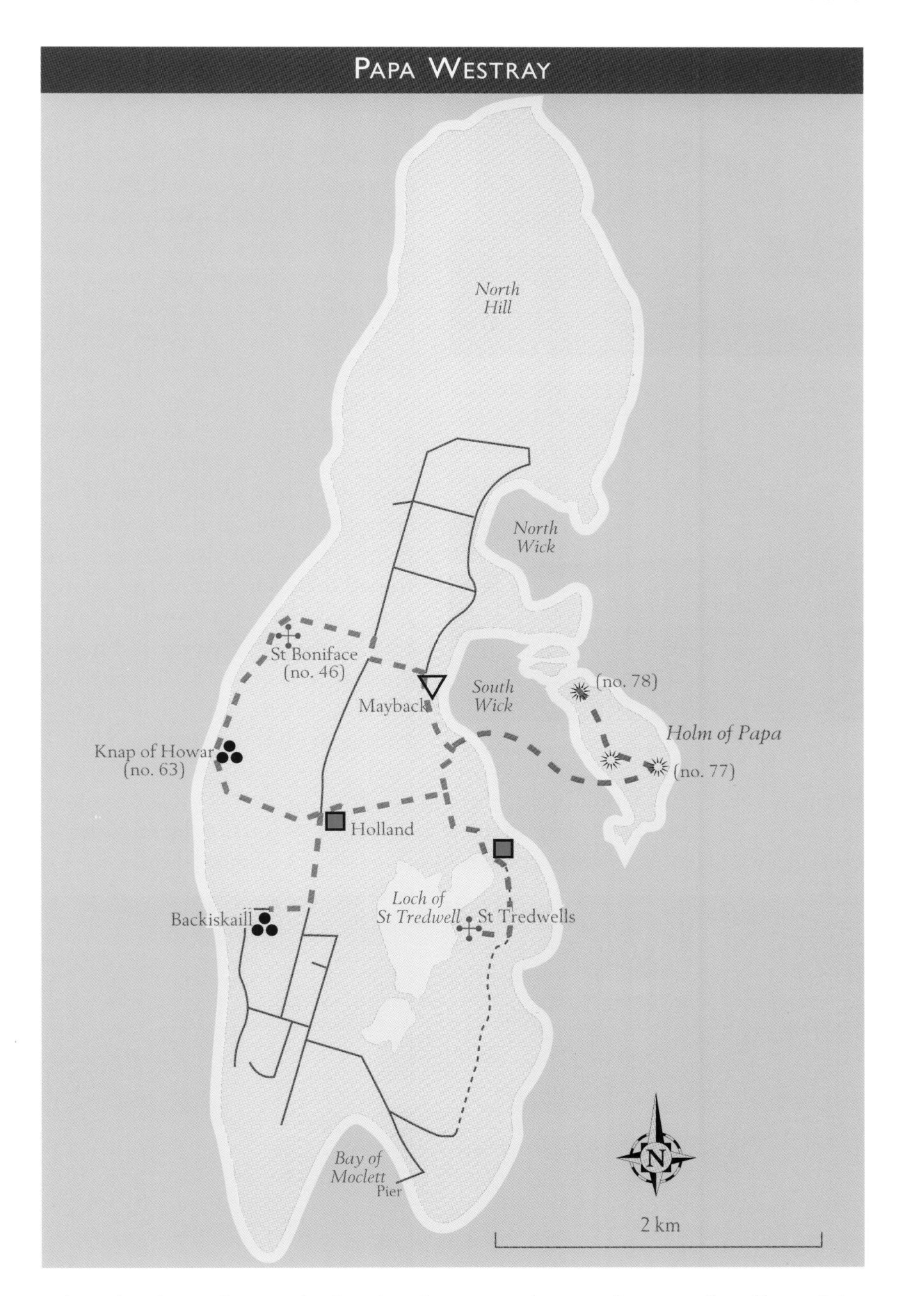

The island can be reached either by air or by sea from Kirkwall, and its monuments are best appreciated on foot, beginning at Holland in the centre of this fertile agricultural landscape (HY 488515). The placename Holland is common in the Northern Isles, and it means simply high land, from Old Norse; here, as on North Ronaldsay, the name was given to the principal farm set on the highest part of the agricultural land.

The farm complex at Holland has several interesting features indicative of its status as the Traill estate farm, including a windmill base in a field in front of the house (HY 489512), a smithy, a lectern-type dovecote, a corn-drying kiln and, unusually for the Northern Isles, a horse-engine house.

The dovecote for Holland House

The horse-engine house that drove the corn-threshing machinery for Holland House

Horse-powered threshing machinery was normally in the open air, but this is a well-built covered horse-gang, a circular structure with a conical flagstone roof (the original spaces between its wall-sections have been built up); the machinery has gone, but originally the horses were harnessed to wooden poles attached to a geared wheel, which turned a shaft running from the horse-shed into the adjacent barn to the threshing machinery. In a small enclosure to the south of the farm buildings are the circular stone bases for haystacks, the stones for each base being neatly gathered into a small cairn between times when the old hay is finished and the new has yet to be stacked. Before leaving the farm, arrange with the owner for a boat-trip to the Holm of Papay later in the day. This can also be arranged through the Papay Community Co-operative at Beltane House, a short distance along the road east of Holland, where a row of farmworkers' cottages has been excellently converted into a shop and guest-house.

A spacious 5000-year old house at Knap of Howar

From Holland, take the signposted track westwards past the dovecote to the neolithic houses near the shore at Knap of Howar (no. 63), their turf-covered walls often bright with sea-pinks.

From here it is a pleasant walk northwards along the shore to Munkerhoose, the site of a broch with external buildings which is under severe erosion by the sea (stonework is visible in the cliff), and the restored church of St Boniface (HY 488526). This church was built in the 12th century as a rectangular nave and chancel, but the nave was extended westwards in the early 18th century in order to insert a loft for the Traill family. The chancel was at some period demolished and its site used as the

Traill family burial enclosure. Two Early Christian cross-incised gravestones have been found buried in the churchyard (one in NMS and the other in Tankerness House Museum), indicating that there was ecclesiastical activity on the site even before the construction of the 12th-century church. Contemporary with the latter is a Norse hogback tombstone (no. 46) still to be seen in the churchyard on the east side of the church.

Follow the track from the church to the main road and return north and almost immediately east along a track to the east shore of the island; walking southwards along the shore you will pass a typical farm mound at Mayback (HY 495524), betraying the centuries over which a single place may be occupied, and a row of seven boat nausts at Skennist (HY 496519), before reaching the pier and the boat for the Holm.

The tiny island is now the home for sheep and a colony of black guillemots, but its archaeology is eloquent witness to former glory in human eyes as well, for there are no fewer than three neolithic chambered tombs. Looking like a grass-covered submarine at the south end is a hugely extravagant Maes Howe type of tomb (no. 77), into which the visitor descends by ladder through the conning tower. At the north end there are the outlines of an excavated stalled cairn (no. 78), while between the two may be discerned the surface traces of the third tomb, probably another stalled cairn (HY 507518). The shell of a building on the west shore was a stable for the ponies formerly kept on the island.

Back on Papay, follow the track southwards to the old corn-mill at Hookin (HY 500512), astride a burn running from the Loch of St Tredwell to the sea. There was once a fine chapel to the Pictish saint, Triduana, on a promontory projecting into the loch on its east side, but little remains to be seen of what was a favourite place of pilgrimage in late medieval times (HY 496508). Between the loch and the Bay of Burland is a well-preserved section of the treb dyke which used to divide the island into two unequal parts (HY 496506-499505), surviving as a broad bank, almost a metre high. Traces of the western section of the dyke may be seen near Backiskaill, where there is also an excellent example of a crescentic burnt mound (HY 485509).

Excavating the north tomb on Holm of Papa Westray

ROUSAY

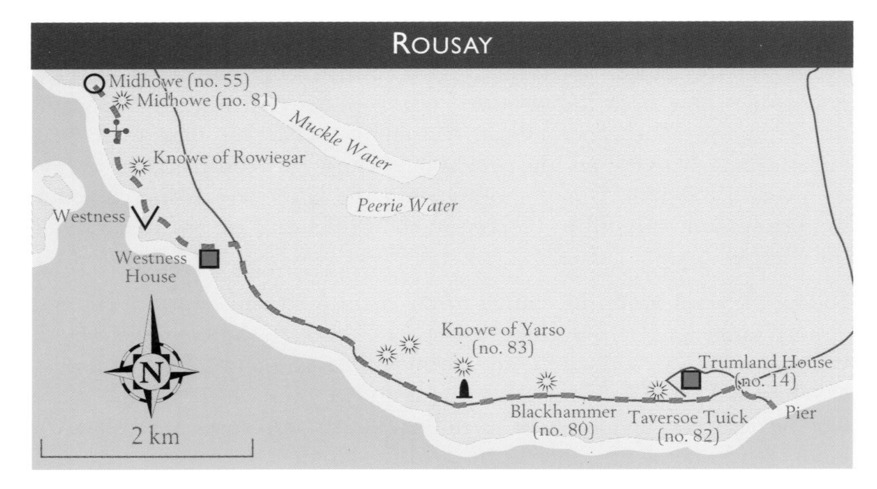

The ferries from Tingwall and Kirkwall come in at Trumland pier in Wyre Sound on the south-east shore of the island and, although it is possible to cover this entire excursion on foot, a more leisurely day will be achieved by taking the mini-bus or a taxi from the pier to Midhowe and walking back. Rousay has a great wealth of archaeological monuments: at least twelve chambered cairns, many cairns, barrows and burnt mounds, eight brochs, an important Viking-age settlement and cemetery at Westness, and a fascinating pre-improvement agricultural landscape at Quandale. The fact that so many prehistoric monuments have been excavated and made accessible and comprehensible to the public is primarily a reflection of the energy and financial generosity of Walter Grant, who lived in Trumland House and was responsible for many excavations in the 1930s. The upland interior of the island rises unusually high for Orkney (250 m OD), and the fertile areas lie along the coast, determining the distribution of both modern and prehistoric settlement.

From the road above Midhowe, follow the signposted path downhill towards the sea - there is a wonderful view across Eynhallow Sound - and enter an unlikely looking hangar to see the chambered tomb of Midhowe (no. 81) as revealed by excavation. A little to the north-west, close to the shore, stands the broch and its outworks (no. 55); the name of Midhowe originally distinguished this broch-mound from one to the north-west (North Howe, HY 370307) and another to the south-east (South Howe, HY 372303), both of which are still visible, though the latter is badly eroded by the sea.

The great lintel over the entrance into the broch of Midhowe (Right)

The cliffs of Scarba Head near Midhowe

Follow the shore southwards to the ruins of the post-Reformation church of St Mary's (the great buttresses were added to the ruin at the end of the 19th century in an attempt to halt its decay), and, at one corner of the churchyard, the foundations of an earlier medieval square stone tower (HY 373301), known as The Wirk. Further south along the shore towards Westness, there are overgrown remains of another stalled cairn, Knowe of Rowiegar (HY 372297), very similar to Midhowe. Continuing along the shore, notice traces of excavations on the site of an important Viking-age farm (HY 375296) with its adjacent cemetery on the low headland of Moa Ness and boat-naust on the south side of the headland (neither cemetery or boat-naust are visible).

A tomb fit for the ancestors at Yarso

Sheltered amongst trees is Westness House (HY 383289), built around 1750 and only supplanted as the grand house of the Rousay estate when Trumland House was built. Walk up the track to the road and continue south-eastwards along the road for almost 2 km. On the natural terraces above the road is an important group of neolithic chambered cairns; Knowe of Lairo (HY 398279) is a long cairn in which a small burial chamber was enclosed at the east end of a cairn almost 50 m long, piled high over the chamber and then tailing away to a low north-west end; the Knowe of Ramsay (HY 400279) was originally a magnificent tomb like Midhowe with fourteen burial compartments but it survives as little more than a low mound; high above is the Knowe of Yarso (no. 83), given an artificial roof after excavation and well worth the climb - as is the view from its vantage point of 100 m OD.

Beside the road is an impressive standing stone about 2.2 m high, known as the Langsteen (HY 404274), and along the road to the east are the signposted and well-preserved tombs of Blackhammer (no. 80) and Taversoe Tuick (no. 82), excavated, as were all the tombs in this excursion, by Walter Grant and his colleagues. A fitting end to the day would be a glimpse of Grant's home, Trumland House (no. 14).

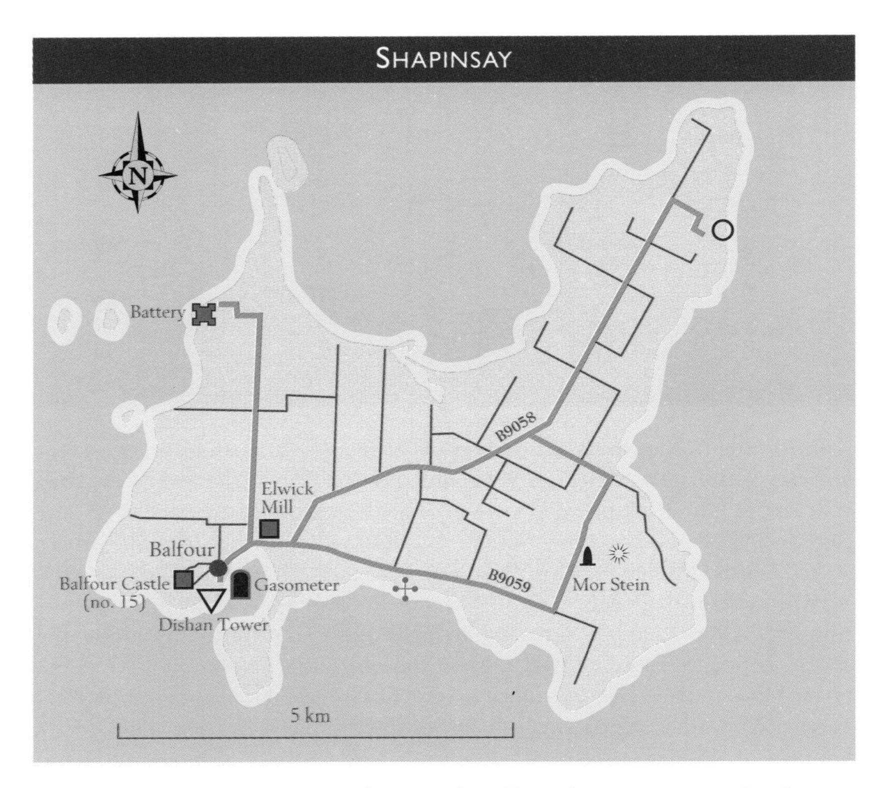

It is easy to take a car across from Kirkwall to Shapinsay, one of Orkney's most intensively farmed islands. A glance at the map or the aerial photograph on p.62 will show immediately the influence of 19th-century ideas about agricultural improvement, with a carefully designed grid of roads and field boundaries. Improvement transformed Shapinsay from a brown peat-covered island to a green island of crops and pasture. As the ferry approaches the pier, it passes an imposing round stone tower known as the Dishan Tower, which was built in the 17th century as a dovecote and converted in the 19th century as a salt-water shower.

The baronial splendour of Balfour Castle

The Dishan Tower offered a discreet salt-water bathe

Balfour village began life as Shoreside, the earliest planned village in Orkney, which was created in the late 18th century soon after the estate was bought by Thomas Balfour. His early attempt at agricultural improvement was swept away by David Balfour's work embracing the entire island some sixty years later. He renamed the village and demolished the southern part of it in the course of building Balfour Castle (no. 15). The Smithy has become a museum and restaurant but retains its forestair and crowstepped gable above the door. At the north end of the village is a stone tower with a red brick parapet which was a gasometer built in the mid 19th century to supply gas to the Castle and village.

The surviving meal mill for the estate was not built until 1883, but it is an unusually large mill of three storeys (HY 485169, beside the B 9059). It was powered by water from a burn running into Elwick Bay, and the overshot wheel and lade are still visible.

From Elwick Bay, take the minor road leading north to Galtness and west to see the World War II Battery (HY 475198). Return south to the B 9059 and take the B 9058 towards the Ness of Ork to visit Burroughston broch (no. 52; signposted). Returning south on the B 9058, take a minor road to the east at HY 516184 to see the Mor Stein, a fine standing stone some 3 m high. Less than 0.5 km to the east is a group of about ten burial mounds. Continue south to the B 9059, turn right and after about 2 km park at the parish church. In the churchyard is a roofless burial aisle, which was formerly attached through an arch in its south wall to an earlier church. The arch bears the date 1656 and the initials M G B for Master George Buchanan, and inside there are mural tablets commemorating members of the Balfour family. Return westwards to Balfour Village.

The broch of Burroughston was the iron-age equivalent of Balfour Castle

St Magnus Cathedral, Kirkwall

MILITARY ARCHITECTURE AND LIGHTHOUSES

The Churchill Barriers between St Mary's Holm, Lamb Holm, Glims Holm and Burray

Orkney holds a special attraction for visitors with an interest in military and naval warfare. When Sir Walter Scott visited Orkney in 1814, he saw in progress the construction of a remarkable military installation at Longhope on the south-east extremity of Hoy. This was the Longhope battery with its attendant twin martello towers of Hackness (no. 3) and Crockness (ND 324934), built to safeguard the Longhope anchorage during the war with the United States of America that had begun in 1812. Longhope was unusual on several counts, not least because it turned out to be a white elephant. Longhope was an essential but highly vulnerable anchorage: essential because it offered shelter from all winds adjacent to the treacherous Pentland Firth and yet was served by four sea approaches between islands, and vulnerable because there was no land-based defence against sea-borne marauders who could decimate the ships at anchor like penned-in sheep. During the American war, Longhope was adopted as the rendezvous anchorage for trading ships bound for the Baltic, which waited for the naval warship that would escort the convoy across the North Sea. They presented a sitting target for the American privateers and the need for their defence was acknowledged and met by the provision of guns mounted on a standard battery and backed up by others mounted on the two martello towers.

The name martello and the idea of such towers had been adopted by Britain after experience of them in Corsica at the end of the 18th century; martello is a corruption of the name of Cape Mortella in Corsica, where English forces captured one of these towers in 1794. With their height and thick walls, martello towers provided an excellent defence against attack from the sea, and no fewer than 103 were built along south-eastern English coasts against the threat of a Napoleonic invasion from France in 1803-5. The invasion threat continued even after the Battle of Trafalgar in 1805, and led to the construction of a martello tower to guard Leith harbour at Edinburgh in 1809 (Longhope and Leith were the only such towers to be built in Scotland).

In the event, the American war was over and Napoleon finally overthrown before the Longhope battery and martello towers were completed; even during the war no American privateer had attempted to attack a convoy at anchorage, preferring to swoop on the open sea. The towers were refurbished to take modern gun mountings in 1866, along with extensive modification of the battery, in response to the threat of Irish-American privateers, but again the threat failed to materialise and the Longhope guns remained silent. In fact, they were never fired in anger. Just once, in 1892, the 68-pounder cannons at Longhope were fired as a peaceful exercise by the Orkney Artillery Volunteers, but they were long obsolete by the First World War.

Access to the top of the Hackness martello tower involved clambering over the rail on which the great gun swivelled

Orkney, especially the anchorage at Scapa Flow, played an important part in both great wars with Germany in the early 20th century, primarily because of her strategic position for intercepting enemy ships bound for the Atlantic but also, in 1939, Orkney was thought to be outside the range of German torpedo-carrying aircraft and therefore a safe base for the British Home Fleet. There are many structural traces of the two wars, from the 'Burma Road' built in Deerness as a military exercise in the early 1940s and leading to a roundabout in the middle of nowhere (HY 593083) to the batteries lining the shores of Scapa Flow and the disused airfields such as that at Twatt, Birsay. Among the most notable relics of the 1914-18 war are the blockships sunk to deter enemy submarines entering Scapa Flow through the eastern approaches, especially those blocking Holm Sound between the islands of Lamb Holm, Glims Holm and Burray. On Marwick Head at Birsay, there is a large memorial to the war hero Lord Kitchener and his men, drowned when the HMS Hampshire was sunk by a mine on June 5, 1916; the square castellated tower was erected by the people of Orkney in 1926 (HY 226251).

Four Royal Naval airship stations were built in Scotland between 1915 and 1916, and one of them was at Caldale on the south flank of Wideford Hill above Kirkwall (HY 413104). The huge sheds had a timber frame covered with corrugated iron, and sliding doors at one end, and a giant windscreen helped in the tricky business of handling airships into the sheds in windy conditions.

The safeguarding of Scapa Flow was again of vital importance in World War Two, highlighted in October 1939 by the sinking of the Royal Oak battleship by a German U-boat that managed to squeeze in past the old blockships. This time the eastern approaches were sealed permanently by the Churchill Barriers, solid obstacles composed of concrete blocks and created by the labour of Italian prisoners-of-war (no. 1). The other marine defences have gone, the booms, mine loops and anti-submarine nets, but the Barriers remain, as road-bearing causeways linking the southern isles.

The batteries on Hoxa Head, South Ronaldsay, are particularly worth a visit (no. 3), and the Scapa Flow Visitor Centre at Lyness in Hoy (no. 4) provides a rounded view of this important anchorage. Guarding the sea-route into Kirkwall are two batteries on the north-west coast of Shapinsay, Galtness Battery (HY 475198) and Castle Battery (HY 481199), both well preserved with gun and searchlight emplacements, ammunition magazines, shelters for personnel and an engine-room.

The Balfour Battery from the air

The Churchill Barrier between St Mary's Holm and Lamb Holm

1 Churchill Barriers

AD 1941-3.

HY 483012-ND 476948. Foundations for sections of the A 961 between St Mary's Holm and St Margaret's Hope, South Ronaldsay.

There are four barriers spanning the sounds between mainland, Lamb Holm, Glims Holm, Burray and South Ronaldsay, a total length of some 2.3 km. They were built during the Second World War with the object of blocking the four eastern approaches to Scapa Flow, as part of an attempt to create a safe anchorage for the British Home Fleet. Massive concrete blocks were made and set in position by Italian prisoners-of-war and, after the war, the barriers were surfaced as a foundation for the modern road. The predecessors of the barriers, the block-ships sunk during the First World War for the same strategic purpose, can be seen alongside.

The first stage in the construction of the barriers was to lay down a rubble base: in some places the water was up to 18 m deep, and it took a quarter of a million tons of stone and rubble to complete the foundation, most of it from a quarry on Lamb Holm. The casting yard for the concrete blocks was at St Mary's Holm, where some 66,000 blocks were made, weighing five or ten tons each, and these were laid on top of the rubble base. The barriers also provide an insight into the results of human intervention in the natural environment, because over the four decades since they were built there has been a massive accumulation of sand against them.

2 Italian Chapel, Lamb Holm

AD 1943-5.

HY 488006. Signposted footpath E from A 961.

The ingenuity and improvisation of the Italian prisoners-of-war who had worked on the Churchill Barriers led to the creation of this small chapel dedicated to Regina Pacis, the Queen of Peace (see p.29). It was designed by Domenico Chiocchetti, an artist and church decorator in peacetime, and consists of two Nissen huts placed end-to-end with embellishments made largely from materials salvaged from the sea. The entrance has an elaborate facade with pinnacles and a bellcote and the colourful interior is divided into nave and chancel by a beautiful wrought-iron screen. Behind the altar is a painting of the Madonna and Child flanked by windows with painted glass, and the entire span of the vault is painted with finely detailed frescoes.

The prisoner-of-war camp was already abandoned by the time that the chapel was finished in 1945 but, outside the chapel, there is a concrete statue of St George slaying the dragon which formerly decorated the camp 'square'. Within its base is preserved a roll with the names of all the prisoners. Through the efforts of local people, the chapel was restored by its chief creator, Domenico Chiocchetti, during a three-week visit in 1960, and it retains today a very special place in Orcadian memory of the last war.

The defence of Scapa Flow: World War II Balfour battery on Hoxa Head (Right)

Hoxa Head, Coastal Batteries, South Ronaldsay

20th century AD.

Hoxa Battery ND 404925; Balfour Battery ND 403930. At the tip of Hoxa Head; take the B 9043 from St Margaret's Hope to Uppertown, and the minor road and track to the end of the peninsula.

Hoxa Head overlooks the main entrance into Scapa Flow through Hoxa Sound. Hoxa Battery was built in the First World War at the southern tip of the peninsula and equipped with 6-inch gun emplacements and magazines. In the Second World War it was rebuilt with two 6-inch gun emplacements and magazines, an observation post, an engine-room and footings for searchlights. These defences were strengthened in 1940-1 by the addition of another battery to the north, alongside the lighthouse built in 1901. This is the Balfour Battery, which is now the better preserved of the two. There are two twin 6-pounder gun emplacements with their ammunition magazines and shelters, an observation tower, three searchlight emplacements and an engine-room.

Scapa Flow Visitor Centre, Lyness, Hoy

20th century.

ND 309946. Signposted from the B 9047 on the E coast of the island.

Orkney Islands Council.

Lyness was the major naval base for Scapa Flow during both World Wars, and it was used by the Royal Navy until 1956. The original oil-pumping station has been renovated and used as an interpretation centre for the story of wartime Scapa Flow. The station was built in 1917 to house the steam-driven pumps that brought oil from tankers moored at the the piers into storage tanks. One of the four tanks survives, designed to hold 12,000 tons of oil. The gleaming pumps were originally powered by coal, but they were converted to oil in 1936, when another twelve storage tanks were built. The displays include artefacts recovered from HMS Hampshire and from ships of the scuttled German fleet.

Pillbox on the slope above Lyness

The naval base at Lyness (Top)

By 1940 there were more than twelve thousand military and civilian personnel at Lyness, and one of the great red sheds built around 1918 was converted into the largest cinema in Europe. Even more striking is the cinema built around 1942 south of Lyness (ND 307922). A huge Nissen hut was transformed by a facade built in art deco style, with its brickwork painted black and bands of white linking the windows (see p.35). The Nissen hut has been demolished and the facade is now a guesthouse.

On the hillside above Lyness are the naval cemetery and a good example of a pillbox, a small defensive look-out post so-called from its squat circular shape.

Hackness gun mounting and parapet

5 Hackness Martello Tower and Battery, Hoy

AD 1815 and 1866.

ND 338912. At the NE end of the South Walls peninsula, side road off the B 9047.

Historic Scotland.

The tower appears to be circular, but the wall on the seaward side is twice as thick as that on the landward side in order to withstand bombardment, and this creates an elliptical plan. Inside, each of the floors is circular. Access into the tower is on the landward side at first-floor level, as a defensive measure; a single doorway, set at a height of about 4 m above ground-level and reached originally by a portable ladder, leads into the living quarters for the gunners and their N.C.O. The tower had its own water-supply from a cistern built into the foundations, and the water could be raised to the living quarters by a hand-pump set into the recess on the left-hand side of the entrance passage. The beds were arranged radially round the wall, and the N.C.O. had the privacy of his own cubicle. Stairs within the thickness of the wall led down to the ground-level storeroom and magazine and up to the parapet and gun platform. At a height of some 10 m above the ground, the top of the tower gives a wide view over the approaches to the Longhope anchorage, and the 24-pounder cannon could also guard the landward side of the battery against any attack from a landing party. The original gun mounting was modified in 1866, and the tower was used as a naval signal-post during the First World War.

Hackness martello tower and gun battery from the air (Right)

Less than 180 m to the north-west of the tower lies the battery, designed as a powerful deterrent with eight 24-pounder guns sweeping the south-east approaches to Longhope through Switha Sound and Cantick Sound. The gunners were protected by a stone parapet and an embankment, while behind the battery were their barracks and stores and a magazine built partially underground, the whole installation enclosed within a high stone wall on the landward side. Most important of the extensive renovations carried out in 1866 was the remodelling of the battery itself to provide heavier guns and better protection for the gunners: four 68-pounder cannons were mounted so as to fire through embrasures rather than simply over the parapet. Additional domestic buildings include, beside the gate, an officers' block which later became a farmhouse. The sandstone used to build both the Hackness and Crockness martello towers and the battery was quarried at Bring Head on the north-east coast of Hoy and transported by boat to Longhope.

LIGHTHOUSES

Measures designed to improve safety at sea have created a range of monuments from major lighthouses to unlit beacons and even cairns of stones that act as navigational markers. Orkney possesses eleven major lighthouses, each consisting of a circular tower to carry the light and low ranges of keepers' accommodation; the latter can be architecturally as interesting as the towers themselves. Hoy High (HY 268060), one of the two lighthouses built on Graemsay in 1851, can boast keepers' houses built in an impressive style that has been likened to Assyrian temples.

By the end of the 19th century, minor, unmanned lights were becoming common, each with a local attendant keeper who paid twice-weekly visits to maintain the light and consisting of little more than a tower - that on the Brough of Birsay, Orkney (HY 234285), built in 1925, is worth visiting in conjunction with earlier monuments on the island (see no. 52).

The lighthouses on North Ronaldsay and Sanday present between them a fascinating visual impression of the way in which early lights developed. The tower on Dennis Head, North Ronaldsay (no. 8), was one of the first four lights built by the Northern Lighthouse Board (the others were on the Mull of Kintyre in Argyll, Eilean Glas on Harris and Kinnaird Head in Aberdeenshire); these early lights had fixed lanterns consisting of a mass of individual lamps each with its own reflector, burning whale oil. The original tower on Start Point, Sanday (no. 6), had no lantern and was only of daytime use, but in 1806 it was fitted with an innovatory `revolving' light, in which the reflector frame revolved by clockwork mechanism. Previously the only way to achieve light visible from more than one direction was to build double lights with twin towers as on the Pentland Skerries, and the new revolving light was less expensive to maintain. Start Point was so successful that the light on Dennis Head was abandoned.

Start Point lighthouse, Sanday, by W Daniell, 1821

6 Start Point, Lighthouse, Sanday

19th century AD.

HY 786435. Start Point is a tidal island at the E tip of Sanday and the lighthouse, although clearly visible from the mainland, can be reached only at low tide on foot across the sand.

The original tower was built in 1802 as an unlit beacon and converted into a revolving light in 1806, but it was rebuilt in brick in 1870. The tower is just over 22 m high and the light was made automatic in 1962. The original keepers' accommodation admired by Sir Walter Scott has survived in good condition alongside the towers; the proportions and overall design of the house and the original tower were particularly fine. Perhaps the most remarkable aspect of the modern lighthouse is the distinctive marking that the tower was given in the early 20th century, when it was painted with wide vertical stripes of black and white, making it impossible in the daytime to confuse the lighthouse with any other.

7 Dennis Head, Lighthouse, North Ronaldsay

AD 1854.

HY 784559. At the end of track leading across Dennis Ness from main road.

Northern Lighthouse Board.

A new lighthouse was built on North Ronaldsay in 1854, almost a kilometre to the north-west of the old beacon. Dennis Ness is so low and flat that an exceptionally tall tower was needed: at a height of 41 m, this is the tallest land-based lighthouse built in the British Isles. In common with othe lighthouses built at a similar period, the tower wa constructed of red brick rather than stone as ar economy measure, and the bricks had to b imported. The tower was given its two broad whit bands of paint in 1889 in order to distinguish it ir daylight.

8 Dennis Head, Lighthouse, North Ronaldsay

AD 1789.

HY 790553. On SE tip of Dennis Head, less than 0.5 km walk over rough pasture from the road near Bewan.

The oldest lighthouse in the Northern Isles, this i a very pleasing stone-built tower some 21 m high. I was built in 1789 as a manned light, but in 1809 i was converted into an unlit beacon and the lanterı was replaced by a great ball of masonry which hac topped the beacon at Start Point, Sanday.

The tower survives in good condition externally, but the timber stairs inside have rotted away; the ruins of the original keepers' house may be seen alongside.

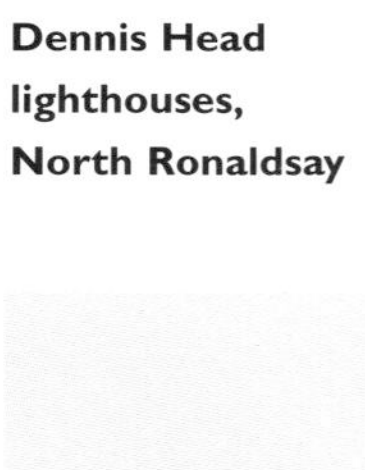

Dennis Head lighthouses, North Ronaldsay

2 HARBOURS AND TOWNS

The waterfront of St Margaret's Hope, with buildings end-on to the sea

While the focus of Orkney's trading activities was around the North Sea, Kirkwall's status as major harbour and town was unassailable, but the development of trans-Atlantic trade in the early 18th century favoured Stromness, more conveniently sited on the west side of mainland. For the ships of the great Hudson's Bay Company, Stromness was their last haven before the long voyage across the Atlantic Ocean, as it was to other merchant ships and whaling ships. Kirkwall maintained its role as the administrative centre of the islands, and, as royal burgh, one of its privileges was a monopoly of foreign trade, but this inevitably became increasingly difficult to uphold in the face of Atlantic competition in Stromness.

Many smaller harbours throughout the islands were of local importance, but only St Margaret's Hope developed into a small town. Even Pierowall failed to develop into a major harbour until modern times, despite its prominence in Viking times as a port of call between Orkney and Shetland. It is perhaps surprising that Pierowall even lacks an extant example of a grain-store, for Orkney's surplus grain was an important export to Shetland and Norway in the 17th century, returning with wool and money from Shetland and timber from Norway. There are imposing grain-stores or girnells on the water-fronts in Kirkwall, St Mary's, Burray village and St Margaret's Hope.

Orkney's participation in the herring boom of the 19th century was never the equal of that of Shetland, but the islands were well placed to benefit from the success of the British Fisheries Society venture at Wick in Caithness. Fish curers soon realised that rents were cheaper in Orkney and that landing dues could be avoided on the islands. The major herring fishing stations were at Whitehall in Stronsay, at Stromness and in Burray and South Ronaldsay, and at the industry's peak in the 19th century a fleet of some four hundred boats could be seen crowded into Papa Sound off Stronsay. Much of the village of Whitehall and its pier were built in the early part of the century to service the herring fleet, the boats coming from all over Orkney and farther afield.

Grain-store at St Mary's

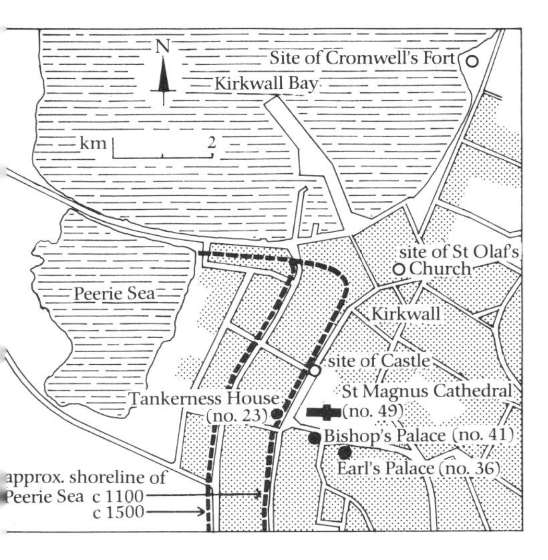

Sheriff Court Building, Kirkwall, by David Bryce

Plan showing the early development of Kirkwall (Top left)

9 Kirkwall

HY 4511.

The modern town of Kirkwall has a long and fascinating history of development that is largely masked by its present appearance. The practical orientation of the town today gives the impression of development on either side of a main street running down to the harbour on Kirkwall Bay, though the bleak and largely modern waterfront should give the game away. The clue lies in the Peerie Sea, now a small loch separated from the the bay by a sandspit known as the Aire but once very much bigger and a natural harbour at the head of the bay: the line running approximately north-south and formed by Albert Street, Broad Street and Victoria Street marks the old shoreline in the medieval period. The process of reclamation of land to the west of that line began very slowly from the 13th century onwards until by 1861 the line of Junction Road marked the contemporary shoreline after 100 m of land had been reclaimed (partly by dumping of rubble and earth and partly by natural build-up of shingle). Today the Peerie Sea has shrunk still smaller and its shore lies some 250 m from the medieval water-front.

To judge by references in *Orkneyinga Saga* and artefacts found in recent excavations, there was Viking-age settlement at Kirkwall (ON *Kirkjuvagr*: church bay) perhaps even before the earliest church was built in the 11th century, but nothing is known of its buildings and it was certainly no urban centre to rival the Norse trading towns of Dublin or York, despite the political importance of the Orkney earldom. Little of the church of St Olaf survives, apart from an attractive carved stone doorway with a round arch, apparently not in its original position but close by, in St Olaf's Wynd off Bridge Street. An 11th-century hogback tombstone was recovered in the early 1970s from the site of St Olaf's churchyard and is now in Tankerness House Museum. The oldest part of Kirkwall, about which least is known, was around and to the north of this church.

Once the building of St Magnus Cathedral was under way from 1137, a second focus of settlement grew up to the south of the first, above the shore of the Peerie Sea. When James III created the royal burgh of Kirkwall in 1486, his charter refers specifically to the two areas of Burgh and Laverock, the former the old town and the latter the diocesan domain around the cathedral. The oldest domestic buildings surviving are parts of the Bishop's Palace (no. 35), begun in the 12th century, and Tankerness House (no. 20), probably of early 16th-century date. Nothing remains of the castle built in the 14th century by the Sinclairs apart from an armorial panel on a later building in Castle Street; it stood on the site of the modern junction between Castle Street, Albert Street and Broad Street, and increasing evidence for the topography of the medieval town suggests that the castle projected out from the shore and was lapped by the sea. It was destroyed in 1615 and its ruins finally demolished in 1865.

The Girnell fronts the harbour at Kirkwall

The Custom House, Kirkwall

Another 16th-century building is the Old Grammar School at no. 36 Broad Street, and there is 16th-century fabric incorporated into other later buildings, especially in Palace Street and Bishop Reid's house in Victoria Street (now nos 48, 50 and 52). It is worth exploring the older streets, for there are many interesting architectural legacies to be seen: Broad Street and Victoria Street contain many 17th-century houses and carved stone fragments. The Girnell (no. 22 Harbour Street), along with the adjacent girnell-keeper's house, was built in the early 17th century as the storehouse for the grain paid as rent in kind to the Earl - the grain was stored in wooden chests or girnells. It is a two-storey building with a basement and two external forestairs. Kirkwall's mercat cross was set up in 1621, originally at the west end of the Strynd but it was moved in the 18th century to the green in front of the cathedral (the original cross is now inside the cathedral and a replica stands outside).

The most spectacular 17th-century building is the Earl's Palace (no. 32), architecturally at least a fitting neighbour to the cathedral even though the means by which it was built, forced labour, must initially have made it a hated symbol of oppression. Earl Patrick was renowned for a regime of violence and disregard for law, but it was based on a sound economy which allowed him to embark on a princely lifestyle and an appropriately ambitious building programme even though that programme was to lead to personal bankruptcy in the end. He inherited the Bishop's Palace and the Castle, useful in themselves as residence and fortification, but the new palace far outshone the old and his completion of the captured castle in Westray (no. 34) was an essay in the best military architecture of the time.

The wealth accrued by Orcadian landowners from the kelp industry allowed the creation of more town houses in the late 18th century, to which families could withdraw from their rural estates to escape the boredom of the long dark winter. The Laing family of Sanday had Papdale House in Berstane Road, a plain but comfortable three-storey house with a pedimented and slightly projecting centre gable. Sir Walter Scott visited this house when he was in Kirkwall in 1814. He was impressed by the Bishop's and Earl's Palaces and by the Cathedral but by little else: 'The town looks well from the sea, but is chiefly indebted to the huge old cathedral that rises out of the centre. Upon landing we find it but a poor and dirty place, especially towards the harbour. Farther up the town are seen some decent old-fashioned houses and the sheriff's interest secures us good lodgings'. To these 'decent old-fashioned houses' were soon added a town house for William Richan of Rapness in Main Street in 1824 (the West End Hotel), Grainbank House in 1829 and Berstane House by David Bryce in 1850.

Adjacent to the Earl's Palace is the Sheriff Court Building, built 1876-7 to a design by the Edinburgh architect David Bryce; by this time Bryce had already successfully completed two major projects in Orkney (Balfour Castle, no. 15, and Trumland House, no. 14), and his confidence was such that initially he had proposed restoring the Earl's Palace itself. The Police Commissioners preferred to build anew - for which we should perhaps be thankful - and the present, fairly austere Sheriff Court Building stands alongside and in pleasant contrast to the earlier ornate residence of the earls of Orkney.

There are carved stones of 16th-century date re-used in the east and west gables, two with the arms of Bishop Robert Reid and one with those of Bishop Edward Stewart.

Notable among other 19th-century buildings are the group of artisans' dwellings built early that century at no. 22 St Catherine's Place (two-storeyed with crowstepped gables) and the Town Hall, built by the Kirkwall architect, T S Peace, between 1884-7 at the corner of Broad Street and St Magnus Lane, with a pilastered entrance in Scots Renaissance style surmounted by the burgh coat-of-arms and statues. Peace also added the tower in 1886 to the episcopal church of St Olaf, designed and built by Alexander Ross in 1875-6 in Dundas Crescent. This interesting church also holds relics of older churches, including an octagonal font from St Mary's in Rousay, aumbreys from the 16th-century St Olaf's Church in Kirkwall and a wooden chancel screen created out of the remains of an early 17th-century episcopal gallery and throne from St Magnus Cathedral. In Albert Street is the charming Custom House, a narrow building with a pilastered main door, which was built in the early 19th century for Captain Balfour of Trenabie in Westray.

There were no substantial harbour facilities until the early 19th century, when two piers forming a sheltered basin were constructed. One of the few industries in Kirkwall to have left tangible evidence is whisky distilling, for the Highland Park Distillery in Holm Road was established in 1798 and flourishes today; most of its distinctive buildings belong to the 19th century with later additions, such as the row of bonded warehouses and the pagoda-roofed kilns.

---

10 Stromness

HY 2508.

Despite the excellent shelter of Hamnavoe, Stromness was slow to develop into a major harbour, in fact it became a burgh only as recently as 1817. There was certainly an inn and the beginnings of a village here in the early 16th century, although nothing now survives of these buildings, and the sheltered anchorage is likely to have been essential to life in the 16th-century

Stromness harbour

Pier Arts Centre, Stromness

mansion at Breckness some 3 km to the west. By the late 17th century there are records of local shipowners in Stromness, but in 1700 there were still only five houses with slate roofs and some less substantial dwellings. Vital to the harbour's development was the decision by the Hudson's Bay Company to use it, perhaps from the early years of the 18th century, as a base for its ships to gather provisions and young seamen in readiness for the long voyage across the north Atlantic. Later that century Stromness also became host to whaling ships en route to the Arctic.

Most of the older buildings along the waterfront today reflect development in the 18th century, when houses and storehouses were built gable-end to the sea, with their own storehouses and piers furnished with post-cranes for loading and unloading the boats. These buildings may be seen along Victoria Street, Graham Place and Dundas Street, a particularly fine example restored as the Pier Arts Centre. Behind John Street at the north end of the town is Millar's House with an unusual moulded stone porch at the front door, its pediment bearing the arms of Millar and Nisbet, the date 1716 and an inscription reading 'Gods providence is my inheritence'.

Alfred Street, Stromness, photographed by Erskine Beveridge in 1894 (Right)

The paved thoroughfare with its archaic air is in fact no earlier than the mid 19th century, and its crooked alignment and variable width reflect its origin as a pathway along the rear of the waterfront buildings, for whose occupants the sea was a vastly more important means of transport. Sir Walter Scott visited Stromness in 1814 and was dismissive: 'Stromness is a little, dirty, straggling town which cannot be traversed by a cart, or even by a horse, for there are stairs up and down, even in the principal streets'. These of course are part of the charm of Stromness today, the narrow alleys and steep steps that lead uphill from the waterfront on to the ridge above the town, the Brinkie's Brae of the Stromness poet and writer, George Mackay Brown.

Stromness lacks the stylish town houses built in Kirkwall by island lairds, and the only 19th-century building of architectural note is no. 97 Victoria Street, built in Italianate style by William Henderson for the Union Bank in 1871 (now the Bank of Scotland).

Stromness Museum at the junction of Alfred Street and South End was built in 1854-8 with the intention that the ground floor should act as a town hall, while the first floor displayed the collections of the flourishing Orkney Natural History Society. The great pile of the Stromness Hotel at the start of Victoria Street was built by Samuel Baikie in 1902. The growth of Stromness in the 18th century was closely connected with the arctic whaling industry and in particular with the Hudson's Bay Company, whose ships not only recruited Orcadian crew but also bought their last fresh provisions before the long haul across the Atlantic. Login's Well (South End) filled the water-barrels of many famous ships, not just of the Hudson's Bay Company but also those of Captain Cook and Sir John Franklin, and the cannon on the seaward side of Ness Road, reputedly taken from an American privateer in 1813, was fired to signal the arrival of Hudson's Bay Company ships. Beyond the Well, at the south end of Ness Road, is a very attractive long building end on to the sea with its own pier; known as Double Houses, this was built in the early 19th century. Nearby Stenigar was a mid 19th-century boatyard before its conversion to a remarkable house for the Orkney artist, Stanley Cursiter, in 1948.

After false starts in the early 19th century, Stromness came into its own with the herring fishing in the late 19th and early 20th centuries. Large herring-boats from Aberdeenshire ports and the Moray Firth crowded into Hamnavoe from mid-May to mid-July, and every pier became a gutting and curing station. But this early season for herring was unreliable, and the herring fishing lapsed as far as Stromness was concerned before the first World War.

Smiddybank gateway, St Margaret's Hope

11 St Margaret's Hope, South Ronaldsay

ND 448935.

This attractive small town lies at the head of a perfect natural harbour, the bay stretching far inland and thus providing excellent shelter. It is thought to have been named after St Margaret of Antioch, although local tradition prefers a link with the Maid of Norway. The seven-year old princess died after crossing the North Sea in 1290, but history fails to record exactly where she died. There is similar uncertainty surrounding an earlier event involving the royal house of Norway. In 1263, King Haakon Haakonsson set off on a punitive expedition to western Scotland, which culminated in the Battle of Largs. After crossing from Norway to Orkney, his fleet sheltered first in Elwick in Shapinsay and then off South Ronaldsay, but scholars are divided over whether the ships lay in St Margaret's Hope or in Widewall Bay to the west. Whichever it was, the king and his men witnessed an eclipse of the sun on 5 August: 'great darkness came upon the sun, in such a way that a small ring was was clear about the outside of the sun; and this continued for about an hour of the day' (*Haakonar Saga*).

The oldest structure surviving is a gateway that once gave access into the courtyard of the 17th-century house of Smiddybank, built by David Sutherland, that preceded the present 19th-century farmhouse. The gateway is surmounted by the Sutherland arms with the dates 1633 and 1693, and above there is a pediment with the figure of a mermaid. The village and harbour of St Margaret's Hope developed in the 18th century, and there are typical two-storey and attic merchants' houses of that date on Front Road, built cheek by jowl with their crowstepped gables towards the sea. Expansion in the 19th century spread southwards with the buildings along Back Road and round Cromarty Square, including a single-storey smithy which has been restored as a museum. St Margaret's Church and its adjacent manse were built in the mid 19th century in Church Road, the school in 1875 and the Bank of Scotland in 1878. Along with neighbouring Burray, St Margaret's Hope blossomed with the herring fishing, but the blocking of Water Sound with wrecks during the First World War removed access from the North Sea. The Hope survived as a port of call for the daily steamer between Stromness and Scrabster until the route was changed, and only the 19th-century pier reminds of busier days in the harbour.

The Old Smiddy, St Margaret's Hope

3 COUNTRY MANSIONS AND DOVECOTES

Orkney's grandest house of the 19th century, Balfour Castle

Orkney cannot boast of any architecture on a scale to match the great stately homes of parts of mainland Scotland, for most of the larger houses are modest both in size and architectural distinction, but in many cases this is amply recompensed by their setting: seascapes that change from calm tranquillity to dramatic turbulence, from clear vistas of distant islands and headlands to the spray-blurred outlines of a land dominated by the sea. The architects responsible for the larger houses made their setting very much part of the overall design, though it is a matter of personal taste whether the elaborate Scottish Baronial style of 19th-century country mansions such as Balfour Castle (no. 15) really suit their landscape. The Balfour family of Shapinsay commissioned the great exponent of Scottish Baronial architecture, David Bryce of Edinburgh, to design not only the family seat on Shapinsay between 1846 and 1850 but also their house near Kirkwall in 1850, although the latter, Berstane House (HY 468103), is a far more modest design. Through Balfour influence on Orkney County Council, Bryce was also commissioned to design Kirkwall Sheriff Court Building in 1872, in which year he designed Trumland House on Rousay (no. 14) for another powerful Orcadian family, this time adopting a Scottish Jacobean theme.

Trumland House was unusual in being an entirely new building, for most 19th- and 20th-century designs involved enlarging an existing house. Indeed most rural houses, great or small, surviving today represent the culmination of structural additions or modifications over the years. It was this sense of blending in with and belonging to the old order that WR Lethaby achieved with outstanding success at Melsetter on Hoy (no. 12) in 1898, where he extended and amalgamated an earlier house and outbuildings; Lethaby was part of the Arts and Crafts movement of the late 19th and early 20th century, in which hand-crafted products and a reverence for local building traditions were essential, and Melsetter House is considered to be one of the most radical examples of these ideals - and the best of Lethaby's own small body of work. It is said that he was so moved by the original Melsetter and its landscape that he tore up the plans that he had designed in London and began afresh. The result was described by May Morris, daughter of William Morris, as `a sort of fairy palace on the edge of the great northern seas'. His client, an industrialist from Birmingham named Thomas Middlemore, also owned the islands of Rysa and Fara, and Lethaby built another smaller house for him at Rysa Lodge (ND 306962) on the east coast of Hoy, overlooking Rysa Bay and the two small islands beyond. Completed in 1902, Rysa Lodge was again an extension of an earlier building, this time a single-storey croft house.

From the air, Shapinsay's improved landscape reveals its grid of fields and roads

It may well have been Lethaby's interest in old buildings that prompted Thomas Middlemore to have the old monastery on Eynhallow cleared of debris; Middlemore owned the island of Eynhallow, and, when the church and its outbuildings were disentangled from later structures in 1897, he and his architect friend Lethaby were present to examine the buildings (no. 52). The party stayed in a timber-built lodge, painted white, which unfortunately no longer exists.

Agricultural improvement

Balfour Castle (no. 15) was part of a successful venture in estate improvement in the 19th century, whereas the story of Graemeshall (no. 13) was one of mistimed improvement by absentee lairds. It was an advantageous marriage rather than the proceeds from an improved estate that led to the building of a new house of Graemeshall in 1874-6. Attempts to improve the estate had begun in 1827 and had to be internally funded, whereas two decades later there were government loans available at low rates of interest. By then there was also a regular paddle steamer service to provide the essential transport for cattle from Orkney to Aberdeen.

Pre-improvement mansions

An elegant Georgian mansion replaced the ransacked old Hall of Clestrain in 1768 (no. 16), but most landowners continued to use and to modify older houses dating from the 16th and 17th centuries. Many of these were plain rectangular buildings of two storeys and an attic, such as Greenwall in Holm, built in 1656 and still massively intact (HY 514014), but Breckness, west of Stromness, was built in an L-shape in 1633 for Bishop Graham (now ruined, HY 224094). The core of Holland House in Papa Westray is also a rectangular house with crowstepped gables, built in the early 19th century but containing 17th-century panelling, perhaps derived from the single-storey wing to the west; a walled garden was created to the east (HY 488515). There was also a liking in the 17th century for the courtyard plan, derived from the design of the grand palaces such as the Earl's Palace at Birsay (no. 33). This led to some very beautiful houses, which have a special affinity with their landscape, such as Langskaill House on Gairsay (no. 18), and which could blend equally well with the Kirkwall townscape in the case of Tankerness House (no. 20).

Dovecotes

In medieval and later times, most landowners of any substance included a dovecote on their estates. Keeping pigeons for the table provided variety of diet and, in the winter, a much-needed extra source of food, and the fact that the pigeons fed indiscriminately off crops in the vicinity was a disadvantage only to poorer neighbours. There is considerable variety of form amongst dovecotes in Orkney, from the beehive shape of that at Hall of Rendall (no. 22), perhaps the earliest unaltered example dating from the 16th or 17th century, to the cylindrical Dishan Tower in Shapinsay (no. 15) and the more common rectangular dovecotes. Several can still be

An unusual three-sided dovecote at Warsetter in Sanday

appreciated within the context of the house and estate to which they belonged, eg Melsetter (no. 12) and Skaill House (no. 17).

In all cases, the dovecote has a single chamber lined internally with small nesting-boxes (usually about 500), which is entered through a ground-level door and by pigeons through small openings in the roof or high up in the walls; there are often projecting string-courses in the external masonry, designed to prevent rats and other predators from climbing the walls. Circular dovecotes had domed or conical roofs, while the rectangular type is often known as the lectern owing to its flat sloping roof (usually facing south) and projecting, often crowstepped, gables. For the most part, the roofs no longer survive, but, apart from those mentioned below, good examples of 17th- and 18th-century dovecotes may be seen at Woodwick (HY 390240), Warsetter, Sanday (HY 630377) and Holland, Papa Westray (HY 488515).

East elevation of Melsetter House, Hoy, by J Brandon-Jones

12 Melsetter House, Hoy

AD 1738 and 1898.

ND 270893. At the S end of Hoy overlooking North Bay and Longhope.

Melsetter House and Rysa Lodge on Hoy are William R Lethaby's sole works in Scotland and among his very few creations anywhere, for he was a theoretician rather than a practical architect. At Melsetter he was able to incorporate both the original house, an L-shaped two-storey building of 1738, and some outbuildings into a mellow and intimate country house with paved courtyard and walled gardens. Moreover he was able to inject into the overall design the magic quality and fundamental symbolism of his architectural ideal; the symbolism appears in tangible form as a star and moon carved from stone and two small heart-shaped windows with stone mouldings on the south gable of the east front of the house. The magic quality was certainly felt by May Morris, daughter of William Morris who had helped to found the so-called Arts and Crafts movement in architecture and interior design: she wrote of Melsetter that it seemed `the embodiment of some of those fairy palaces of which my father wrote with great charm and dignity. But, for all its fitness and dignity, it was a place full of homeliness and the spirit of welcome, a very loveable place'.

May Morris was a friend of Theodosia Middlemore, wife of the industrialist who had bought the Melsetter estate and herself an embroideress and weaver. Both Middlemores were appropriate patrons for an idealist like Lethaby and with Melsetter they had provided him with a perfect stimulus. He adopted local traditions of building, harling the exterior walls, using local red sandstone for dressings and Caithness flags for the roof and featuring crowstepped gables, but adding his own distinctive mark, particularly on the three gables of the garden elevation. The gables are capped with a rose, a heart and a thistle, above T M T for Thomas, Middlemore, Theodosia, and the date 1898. The entrance hall is dominated by a great sandstone chimney-breast, where a finely moulded fireplace is surmounted by five stone corbels designed as rests for candles which would throw into dramatic relief the row of seven coats of arms carved into the stonework above. The visual effect was enhanced by tapestries and silken wall-hangings, some of which were made in the Morris workshop.

Melsetter House, east elevation

The south wing of Lethaby's house is the original 18th-century house with its vaulted morning room, and a contemporary square dovecote was incorporated into the south-west corner of the old walled garden, balanced by a Lethaby tea-house on the south-east corner. He also adapted an 18th-century outhouse into a chapel, dedicated to St Colm and St Margaret in 1900 and using fine contemporary stained glass. Above the door are carved a sun, a cross and a moon to symbolize Christ as Lord over the heavens, and the east gable is surmounted by a cross carved as an anchor, as a metaphor of the church as the ship of salvation.

Graemeshall, with the 17th-century arch on the right

Trumland House
(Bottom)

13 Graemeshall, Holm

AD 1874-6.

HY 487017. Beside the B 9052 0.5 km NE of the start of the first Churchill Barrier (privately owned museum).

Despite the misfortune of the estate in attempting premature improvement in the early 19th century, the house of Graemeshall today is a gracious mansion in the Scottish style, set in tranquil grounds. It is a double block of two storeys and an attic, with crowstepped gables and mullioned windows, and it was the work of John A Bruce of the Kirkwall firm of Peace Architects. The garden wall retains a moulded arch from the earlier 17th-century house, which was designed round a courtyard and incorporated elements going back to the 15th century. This earlier house was originally called Meall but was renamed Graemeshall after it had been acquired by the Graham family in the mid 17th century.

A chapel to St Margaret of Antioch and Scotland was added to the east wing of the 19th-century house in 1898, and it contains an important early Christian graveslab from Holm parish graveyard. The garden is dominated by large statues of Faith, Hope and Charity created in 1868 for a building (since demolished) in Inverness.

14 Trumland House, Rousay

AD 1872-3.

HY 428277. Close to the SE coast of Rousay, 1 km from Brinyan pier.

An unusually sheltered spot was chosen for this house, a small valley through which a burn runs down to the sea and where it has been possible to coax woodland to grow. Previously the family seat of the Traill family of Rousay was the 18th-century Westness House (HY 383290), but, after his marriage, Lt Gen Frederick W Traill Burroughs decided to commission the celebrated architect, David Bruce, to design a more imposing residence. The result was a mansion in the Scottish Jacobean style, three storeys high with an attic. The first owner's initials and the date 1873 are carved on a panel above the rear door.

The extraordinary gateway over the path leading to the kitchen-garden is built of sculptured stones found in the vicinity of St Mary's Church and the Wirk (HY 373302; see Rousay excursion). They are high quality architectural fragments, carved of red sandstone, some of 13th-century date and some of 16th-century date, and it is thought that the 13th-century pieces may have been 'spares' from St Magnus Cathedral. More architectural fragments are built into the east end of the later St Mary's church, and others were found in the debris of the monastery on Eynhallow (no. 44).

The entrance archway into Trumland's home farm is crowned by a tower with a dovecote incorporated into its steep pyramidal roof.

Balfour Castle

The gateway into Balfour Castle
(Left)

The garden arch at Trumland
(Top left)

15 Balfour Castle, Shapinsay

Mid 19th century AD.

HY 474164. About 1.5 km W of the pier; ferry from Kirkwall.

Between 1846 and 1850, David Bryce designed his first large commission for David Balfour of Shapinsay: his remit to enlarge the existing family house overlooking the sheltered bay of Elwick. It was an invitation to design on a lavish scale, and accordingly Bryce created an outstanding example of a country mansion in Scottish Baronial style, with a square castellated tower rising above the main entrance, further embellished with a corner turret, with huge bay windows to the public rooms, square turrets with pyramidal roofs, round turrets with conical roofs, crowstepped gables and a glorious conservatory almost as large as the drawingroom. The main stair remained in the central, older portion of the now Z-shaped house, but, typical of such Bryce designs, the public rooms are served by an immensely long and broad corridor into which the new main entrance opens.

Part of the village was demolished to improve the approach to the house, and Bryce designed an imposing entrance into the grounds, which consists of an archway with a mock portcullis and flanking lodges, the whole gateway capped by a corbelled parapet. The terraced gardens were laid out by Craigie Halkett of Cramond, Edinburgh, and they include an elaborate 17th-century gateway. This belonged to an earlier house that was burned down by Hanoverian soldiers in 1746 and replaced by the L-shaped building incorporated into Bryce's grand design. It suits well the Baronial style of the later mansion. A moulded archway is flanked by columns and topped with a pediment bearing an armorial panel, the whole composition richly decorated: mermaids holding harps, men and animals playing musical instruments, and, flanking the armorial panel, unicorns and caryatid figures in

The Dishan Tower

17th-century costume. The coats of arms and initials are those of Arthur Buchanan and Margaret Buxton and are identical to those at Carrick House on Eday (no. 19), though the date here is 1674, twelve years later than the Carrick panel.

Another legacy from the 17th century is Dishan Tower, a circular dovecote now somewhat oddly situated on the rocky foreshore, which was restored equally oddly in the 19th century as a 'douche-house', taking advantage of its proximity to the sea to provide a salt-water shower. This too is embellished with a corbelled and crenellated parapet and a crowstepped cap-house.

A gasometer served the needs of Balfour Castle and village in the 19th century

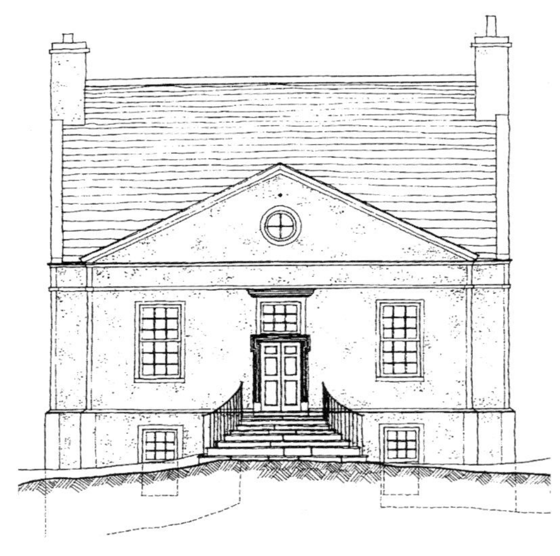

Reconstruction drawing of Hall of Clestrain by Simpson & Brown Architects
(Top right)

16 Hall of Clestrain

AD 1768.

HY 296073. Between the A 964 and the shore, some 5 km S of Bridge of Waithe near Stromness.

Clestrain was part of the vast estates of the Honeyman family, and the original house was ransacked by the infamous pirate, John Gow, in 1725 (see no. 19). It was replaced in 1768 by an entirely new Georgian mansion, built for Patrick Honeyman, third laird of Graemsay, the island overlooked by the more conveniently located house. It consists of three floors, with a broad projecting centre bay which contains the entrance into the middle floor, framed by moulding and approached by a stair. This central bay was probably topped by a pediment to balance the steep roof, as shown in the reconstruction drawing, but, at the time of writing, the house is sadly derelict. The public rooms are likely to have been on the middle floor, with bedrooms above and the kitchen and family rooms in the basement. There were low pavilions on either side of the house, linked to it by walling, but only one pavilion survives.

17 Skaill House, Sandwick

17th century AD and later.

HY 234186. From Stromness N on the A 967, take the B 9056 to Sandwick.

As it stands today, Skaill House is rather closer to the sea than it was two hundred years ago: a map drawn in 1772 shows the house exactly half-way between the Bay of Skaill and the freshwater loch of Skaill, quite close to the burn running from the loch into the sea. The size and shape of the bay has changed over the centuries, amongst other things leading to the discovery of the prehistoric settlement of Skara Brae (no. 61), and it was clearly proximity to a source of freshwater that determined the location of the house. The same map shows the house as a single block with outbuildings, and the oldest part of the house surviving today is indeed a rectangular block, with the original entrance facing southwards and inland rather than towards the sea, and this, the old Hall of Skaill, is likely to date from the early 17th century when the estate belonged to Bishop George Graham.

Since then there have been considerable additions and alterations: the old Hall and its outbuildings linked by a screen-wall to create a typical courtyard complex as at Langskaill on Gairsay (no. 18), and then another block parallel to the Hall and linked by a short central block to form an H-shaped mansion on the south side of the courtyard. The gable-ends of the two wings of the mansions were later linked by short screen-walls, so that the west side of the entire complex is now one long facade consisting of three gable-walls and two screen-walls with gateways. Various pieces of stone-carving have been re-used over the two gateways and on the modern porch on the east side of the house, including an armorial panel from Bishop Graham's ruined Breckness House near Stromness, an early 17th-century house owned then by the same Graham family that owned Skaill. There is also a rectangular 18th-century dovecote at one corner of the extensive gardens. The ruins of a water-driven meal mill built for the estate in the 18th century stood on the shore of Skaill Bay until the 1980s, when coastal erosion finally completed its demolition.

The south front of Langskaill House

Skaill House (Top)

18 Langskaill House, Gairsay

17th century AD.

HY 434219. Close to the SW shore of the island.

Gairsay is a very attractive small island with a sheltered anchorage in Millburn Bay, and it is not surprising that it was part of a prestigious Norse family estate in the 12th century, conveniently situated as it is astride one of the approaches to the bays of Firth and Kirkwall. *Orkneyinga Saga* tells of the exploits of the Viking Svein Asleifarson who farmed on Gairsay, raided in the Hebrides and Ireland and owned another estate at Duncansby in Caithness, and tradition would locate the remains of his great hall beneath the present Langskaill House.

The east range of Langskaill House

Decorative arch and gun-loops, Langskaill House

The east range of the present house may belong to the house recorded here in the 16th century, which was extended in the 1670s after the marriage of Sir William Craigie of Gairsay and Margaret Honyman, daughter of the Bishop of Orkney. Their initials are carved on a lintel over the entrance to the east range of the house. The original design consisted of three such ranges round a courtyard, with a screen-wall across the fourth side, but the north range has been demolished, the west range is derelict and only the east range, restored in about 1900, remains habitable. This is now a single-storey building with an attic, but the south end at least must at one time have been a storey higher, matching the west range, so as to allow access to the parapet along the screen-wall. Although the building was much altered in the early 20th century, two very fine fireplaces survive on the attic floor, with moulded and carved stone jambs and lintels.

The south front gives a marvellous impression of the fortified and yet elegant family house. The screen-wall with its central gateway is flanked to either side by the gable-ends of the east and west ranges, and a moulded stone base-course runs the entire length of the front. The gateway was originally the only means of access to the house, and it is guarded on either side and above the gun-loops as well as by the parapet. The door itself does not survive, but the slots for the bar that could be drawn across behind the door still exist within the wall on either side. The archway is finely carved with a vine scroll, and on the parapet above there is an elaborate armorial panel crowned with a triangular carved pediment. This was originally even more elaborate, and the rest of the parapet bore a stone balustrade - the whole design must have been very impressive. A similar 17th-century gateway survives in the grounds of Balfour Castle on Shapinsay (no. 15).

Carrick House in the late 19th century

19 Carrick House, Eday

AD 1633.

HY 566384. Close to the shore at the N end of the island, some 11 km from the main ferry pier at Backaland.

This house is perhaps more notable for its historical associations than for its architecture, but its setting is superb and its view over Calf Sound unrivalled. In its original form in the 17th century, it consisted of a typical two-storeyed laird's house with crowstepped gables and a courtyard enclosed by a stone wall, and the gateway, set on the seaward side because most contemporary visitors would arrive by boat, retains its original moulding and arch, with the date 1633 carved on the keystone of the arch.

Above the gateway is an armorial panel with the initials of Arthur Buchanan and his English wife, Marjory Buxton and the date 1662; the same initials and coats of arms appear on the 17th-century gateway in the grounds of Balfour Castle on Shapinsay (no. 15). The original owner and builder of the house was John Stewart, Earl of Carrick and brother of Earl Patrick Stewart, who had been granted the entire island in 1632. Since the 18th century, Carrick House has been famous for its part in the capture of the notorious pirate, John Gow, whose exploits inspired Sir Walter Scott's novel *The Pirate*; in his ship, the 'Revenge', Gow ran aground on the Calf of Eday during an attempt to raid Carrick House in 1725, and he was held prisoner in the house before being sent to London for trial. His ship's bell is still preserved at the house.

20* Tankerness House, Kirkwall

16th-17th century AD.

HY 448108. On Broad Street, almost opposite St Magnus Cathedral; now a museum.

This attractive building is widely regarded as one of the finest early town houses surviving in Scotland, and it has been restored and converted into a museum without losing its essential character. Its present name originated in the 17th century when it became the town residence of the Baikie family of Tankerness, but in the previous century it was the subchantry and archdeanery for St Magnus Cathedral, and the initials of an archdeacon appear on the armorial panel over the entrance gateway: M G F for Master Gilbert Fulzie.

This gateway and the north wing of the house are of 16th-century date, and the panel over the gateway bears the date 1574, and the initials of Fulzie's wife, Elizabeth Kinnaird. The jambs and arch are heavily moulded and the armorial panel is set into a corbelled parapet. The north wing has two storeys and an attic, and the original spiral stair is housed in a small projecting tower just inside the gateway. Subsequent additions and modifications have created the harmonious courtyard house of today, its almost square courtyard entirely enclosed by buildings. On the west side of the house is a peaceful garden, which is graced by a large architectural fragment from the cathedral.

Tankerness House, Kirkwall

21 Tafts, Quandale, Rousay

16th century AD.

HY 373325. From the pier, take the B 9064 along the S and W coast of the island to the N moorland; park at about HY 382324 and walk W and downhill for almost 1 km.

This ruined building is thought to be the oldest two-storey house in Orkney, for its existence is recorded in 1601. It is a plain stone structure with crowstepped gables and double-splayed windows. There were two rooms on the ground floor, separated by a cross-passage, and a stair led from one of them to the two rooms on the upper floor. As at Corrigall (no. 23), the dwelling house was separate from its outbuildings, here consisting of a barn with a corn-kiln and a byre lying alongside the house. The term taft or toft means simply a house and its immediate surroundings, and this building was once the principal house in the crofting township of Quandale. Although Tafts was renovated in the early 19th century, all sixteen households in the township were cleared to make way for sheep in 1845, the worst example of total clearance in the name of 'improvement' that Orkney suffered.

Some 400 m to the south-south-east at HY 374321, there is a well-preserved example of a crescentic burnt mound (see chapter 8); excavation has revealed a rectangular stone setting.

22 Hall of Rendall, Dovecote

17th century AD.

HY 422207. Near the farmhouse of Breck of Rendall on E coast of mainland, minor road to E from A 966, almost 11 km NE of Finstown.

Orkney Islands Council.

This attractive beehive dovecote with its four external string-courses is unique in the Northern Isles. The nests for the pigeons are simply irregular gaps left in the rough masonry of the internal wall-face.

Dovecote, Hall of Rendall (Right)

4 FARM STEADINGS AND RURAL INDUSTRY

Farm steading, Hall of Setter, Hoy, photographed by Erskine Beveridge around 1890

There is a fascinating heritage of traditional rural buildings to be found in Orkney, which not only promotes an understanding of island life over the last couple of centuries but also conveys a strong sense of continuity from early times. This is not necessarily the strict continuity of customs handed down through the centuries but the indirect continuity of farmers and fishermen reacting in the same way to their environment, meeting the same problems with similar solutions, and in particular handling local building materials to the common best advantage. It is possible to find parallels for features seen in the old farmhouses of the 18th and 19th centuries among the excavated remains of Viking-age or prehistoric houses, but ideas can be re-introduced or re-invented, and there is a real obstacle to proving genuine continuity of tradition in the unavoidable fact that we know virtually nothing about the homes of ordinary people between about AD 1300 and 1700, apart from the occasional historical reference.

The idea of the longhouse or byre-dwelling, in which people and domestic animals live under one roof, seems to have evolved in late Norse times, and it can be seen among the surviving farmhouses of the 18th and 19th centuries. Although Corrigall has been restored to its mid 19th-century state with a separate byre, the dwelling-range originally included a byre at one end (no. 23), like Mossetter (no. 24). Dating evidence is insufficiently precise to show whether the difference between the longhouse and the dwelling with separate byre is simply chronological or whether it reflects social status, but certainly by the mid 19th century a separate byre was more normal, sometimes built at right angles to the dwelling but usually parallel to it.

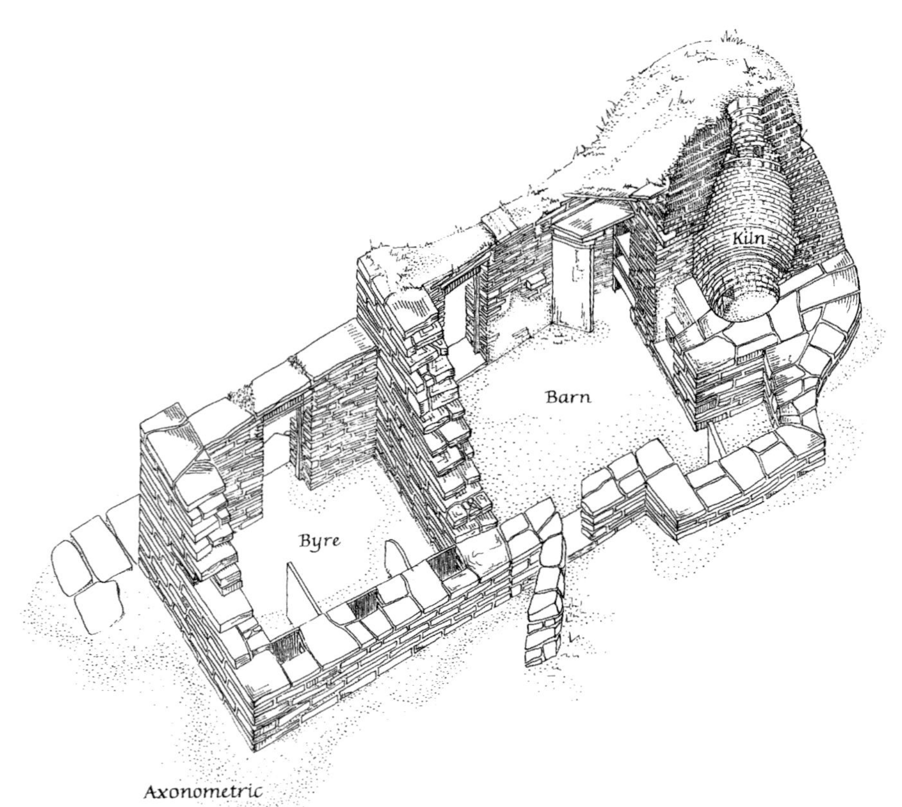

A barn with corn-drying kiln

Other buildings on a small farm might include a stable for ponies, various storehouses and a barn with a corn-drying kiln. Such barns often incorporate a pair of opposing doors in the long walls, through which a draught could be created for winnowing the grain, separating the grain from the chaff, and a clay threshing floor. The object of drying the grain was to make it easier to grind, and this was done in the tall circular kilns that are such an attractive feature of many old farms. The method used can be appreciated particularly well at the two croft museums (nos 23 and 25). Externally such a kiln is beehive-shaped, narrowing towards the open top, but internally the base narrows as well, and the whole structure could be more than 4 m high. From within the barn, there were two openings into the kiln: the main access to the wooden drying floor, where straw across the wooden spars provided a shelf for the grain, and a flue from the fire area below, where peats were laid to create a steady but not roaring source of heat. Each batch of grain would take 6 to 8 hours to dry.

The larger estate-farms were more complex. An excellent example is Holland in Papa Westray, which is still a working farm but where many of the older buildings have been preserved (this has been included in the Papa Westray excursion). West of Holland House are the estate manager's house, the smithy and the joinery, the dairy with a bothy for farmworkers above, the stallion house still with its flagstone roof, a long range with the threshing barn and its mill tramp or horse-engine shed at one end, hay barn and grain lofts in the middle and stable at the other end. Other buildings include the corn-drying kiln, dovecote and windmill base.

Mill of Eyrland

Watermills

A single example of an intact horizontal watermill survives at Dounby (no. 28), but the foundations of another have been excavated at Orphir (no. 39). These mills are small, rectangular drystone buildings, normally windowless and with one door, roofed with flagstones and turf or thatch. They are known as horizontal mills because their water-wheels are set horizontally rather than vertically, and their mechanism is very simple, to the extent that they are really no more than water-powered hand-querns. The two millstones are set at floor-level in the meal-house, the upper stone rotated by the water-wheel or tirl in the under-house below; the tirl consisted of an iron-bound wooden shaft set with inclined wooden blades or feathers, usually eight to twelve in number, and the remains of the tirl can still be seen in many ruined mills in Shetland, though the fittings of the meal-house above have usually been removed.

Such mills were never as common in Orkney as in Shetland, for topographical reasons, and Orkney's few good water-courses were early on harnessed by vertical mills serving larger numbers of customers. Documentary evidence shows that there were mills at least as early as the 15th century; they would normally be demolished and re-built on the same spot, and Boardhouse in Birsay is unusual in retaining a sequence of mills (no. 27). Horizontal mills are sometimes known as Norse mills, but there is no evidence to prove a Scandinavian origin for them and an earlier Irish influence is more likely. The remains of a number of Irish examples have been found in water-logged conditions with preserved timber parts, and tree-ring dating of the wood has shown them to be of Dark-Age date between AD 630 and AD 926. The excavations at Orphir have demonstrated that the type existed in Orkney at least as early as the 10th century.

In the Northern Isles, horizontal mills have also been known as click mills or clack mills because of the distinctive sound that they made during operation. The meal was fed into the millstones from a wooden hopper and shoe suspended above, and it was jiggled gently from the shoe or feed trough into the millstones by a clapper; this was usually a stone on the end of a string attached to the shoe which rattled along on the moving millstone, though at Click Mill, Dounby (no. 28), the clapper is a wooden tongue which is struck by a wooden knob on the millstone at every revolution.

Equally interesting are the external arrangements made to manage the flow of water into the mill, for each had its own stone-lined lade upstream feeding into a timber chute that directed the water on to the water-wheel, and at the head of the lade the sluice had a wooden gate which could be slotted into position to close the sluice and divert the water.

There are several well-preserved mills with vertical wheels, built in the 19th century. The internal machinery can still be seen at Tormiston (no.26) and Boardhouse (no. 27), and, although it is not open to the public, the Mill of Eyrland can be admired from the road as a very successful example of a mill converted into a home without losing the character of the mill (HY 294097; built around 1862).

Peckhole windmill by T S Peace

Windmills

While the small water-driven mill was specially suited to Shetland's steeply rushing burns, windmills were common in Orkney where good water-courses were few but the low-lying windswept landscape ideal for harnessing wind-power. The old windmills went out of use some years ago, but this natural source of power has been harnessed again in recent years,

Windmill base, Holland, Papa Westray
(Left)

with the erection of several wind turbine power generators, such as those on Burgar Hill, Evie (HY 341260) and at Berriedale in South Ronaldsay (ND 459938).

The older windmills are of the type known as the post mill, the simplest form of windmill known to have existed in Britain from at least as early as the 13th century, though none of the surviving remains in Orkney can be dated earlier than the 18th century. The timber superstructure of the mill revolved upon a conical stone-built `post', and it is this stone base that survives today. The fine drawing by T S Peace of a windmill in North Ronaldsay (no. 30) enables us to reconstruct the original appearance of such mills: four sails were fitted vertically to the timber mill-house, and a long tail-beam allowed the whole superstructure to be moved round to face the wind. Here the tail-beam is fitted with a wheel to make its movement easier, and the ladder providing access to the mill is attached to the tail-beam as well. The furled canvas sail attached to each wooden-framed sail is visible, along with the simple rigging that allowed the miller to set the sails, and the close relationship between such windmills and the principles of sailing ships is obvious.

Ancient Dykes

Field boundaries have been constructed since very early times, and Orkney and Shetland have examples going back to the 3rd and 4th millennia BC. More substantial turf and stone dykes were built as territorial boundaries and as agricultural barriers between upland grazing and cultivated land or even, on North Ronaldsay (no. 31), to confine sheep to the foreshore away from the cultivated interior of the island. The two treb dykes of North Ronaldsay may be ancient territorial boundaries. On the whole, the latter type of massive dyke appears to be considerably older than the hill-dykes, even though their local terminology sometimes makes the distinction confusing. Treb dykes in Orkney may also be known as gairsties. They are difficult to date, but the fact that they appear to be earlier than tunship divisions, which may themselves relate to pre-Norse land divisions, has led to the suggestion recently that they might originate in the first millennium BC.

Rural Industry

There are few monuments surviving by which the various rural industries of Orkney may be traced. In the Eday excursion, attention has been drawn to the remains of the 17th-century saltworks on the Calf of Eday, more because they are very unusual than because they are either well-preserved or typical monuments. Salt was normally made in small quantities in a domestic context by evaporation over the kitchen fire.

Another product of the sea was for a time a vital factor in Orcadian economy: seaweed. This was gathered in vast quantities, dried and then burned in shallow pits until it became a boiling liquid; when the liquid cooled and hardened, it could be raised as a solid whole and broken into lumps ready for transport and sale as kelp, a valuable source of iodine and potassium salts. Kelp production was specially suited to Orkney with its shallow seas and prolific growth of seaweed. The 18th and early 19th centuries were the heyday of kelp-making, when it was used extensively in the production of glass, soap and dyes, but it continued on a minor scale into this century. Most of Orkney's kelp was sent to Newcastle and Leith, but it was also exported to west-coast ports such as Dumbarton, Liverpool and Bristol. Many Orkney lairds made huge profits from kelp, but their tenants who were the kelp-makers benefited little.

The over-grown remains of kelp-burning pits can be seen in many places round the shores of Orkney: they were circular, about 1.5 m in diameter and 0.6 m deep, lined and paved with stones. There is a group of very well-preserved pits on the Crook Beach in the northern part of Sanday (HY 679459).

Kelp-burning chimneys on Papa Stronsay

Stronsay led the way in the development of the kelp industry in Orkney in 1721, and there are good examples both of kelp pits and kelp-drying stances on Grice Ness near the cairn (no.70) and on Lamb Ness, near the broch (no. 54). Remains of a more sophisticated approach to kelp-burning may be seen on the small island of Papa Stronsay, across Papa Sound from Whitehall, where there are two stone-built chimneys nearly 2 m high (HY 662296).
Linen manufacture and straw-plaiting for bonnets were also important rural industries during the 18th and early 19th centuries, but they have left no trace on the ground and indeed most of the flax and straw was imported.

Planticrues are a more familiar element in the man-made landscape in Shetland than in Orkney, but there is a particularly well-preserved group at Holms of Ire in Sanday (HY 649459). These small stone-walled enclosures could be square or circular (both are present in Sanday), and they were designed to protect young vegetable plants from the devastating effects of high winds.

Corrigall Farm Museum: byre, stables and barn

Byre and dwelling, with cheeses maturing on shelves beside the door (Top left)

3* Corrigall Farm Museum

8th-19th centuries AD.

Y 324193. On the A 986 between Dounby and the nction with the A 965 Kirkwall to Stromness road, ke a minor road near Harray Stores eastwards; gnposted.

'he range of buildings belonging to this steading ate from the mid 18th century, and they have been eautifully restored to evoke a strong sense of rming life in the mid 19th century (the farm was habited until the mid 20th century, when its otential for the creation of a rural museum was cognised, and it was bought by Orkney County Council). Not only has the fabric of the buildings een restored, but they have also been furnished ith contemporary fittings and equipment typical f 19th-century life - you are likely to find a esident hen, to see Orkney cheeses maturing and sh drying, and to smell the peat burning on the earth. In 1981, the museum won the Award of the ssociation for the Preservation of Rural Scotland is a particularly fine example of restoration work a rural setting'.

'he three major buildings form a close-knit group unning parallel to each other, with paving between em: the dwelling range, a barn and stable range nd a separate byre. It is likely that the west end of e dwelling was originally a byre, but, by the mid 9th century, it had become a parlour with adjacent itchen, living room and bedroom. The byre is rnished with stone partition-slabs, forming stalls, nd a central drain, accommodating the cattle over e winter. The original stable for the native small horses is attached to the south side of the barn, with a manger built into the wall at either end, but the adoption of larger work horses in the 19th century led to the provision of a larger stable at the east end of the barn, which has timber-built stalls. The barn itself was primarily concerned with the preparation of grain for grinding into flour: a clay floor where the grain was threshed, opposing doorways to create the through-draught for winnowing, and a circular kiln for drying the grain. All the roofs consist of flagstones on a timber frame, covered with an insulating layer of turf.

The steading is well placed, with the Burn of Corrigall nearby to provide a source of water not only for domestic use but also, by the later 19th century, for a separate threshing mill powered by a water-wheel, the water for which was carried in an unusual aqueduct over the burn.

24 Mossetter, Farm Steading

18th century AD.

HY 390197. About 5.5 km N of Finstown on the A 966, take a track E towards the Loch of Brockan or less than 1 km, then fork to the N.

This farm was abandoned around 1920, and it is now roofless, but it has some interesting features typical of older longhouses. It was built as a three-roomed house on a slope, with the byre at the downhill, western end, and the bedroom at the uphill end, and it was formerly roofed with flagstones and turf. There appear to have been only two small windows, both in the south wall of the bedroom.

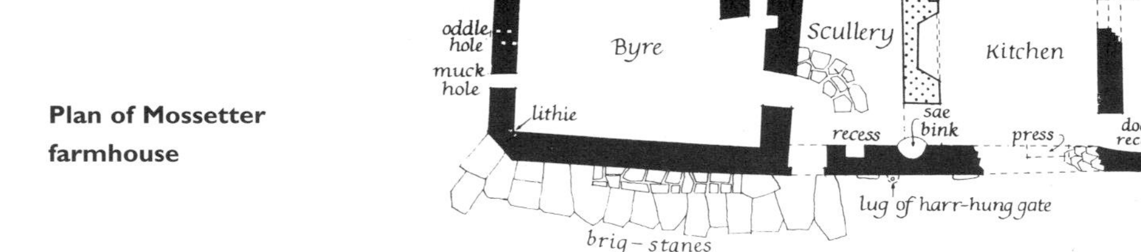

Plan of Mossetter farmhouse

Family and beasts used the same entrance, and a low curving stone wall directed the cattle into the byre rather than allowing them into the dwelling; the byre has lost its slab partitions, but both oddle-hole and muck-hole survive in the west end-wall. The central living-room has been divided into scullery and kitchen by an inserted chimney-wall, and the west gable of the bedroom has another fireplace. Along the north wall of the house there projects an outshot, running the length of scullery and kitchen and overlapping the bedroom, providing neuk-beds and, in the bedroom, a peat-neuk. The two neuk-beds in the kitchen are divided by an upright slab with horizontal corbelling above, a feature very reminiscent of the internal divisions in the broch at Midhowe (no. 55) and underlining the continuity of building traditions. Similarly archaic features are the recesses built into the south wall of the scullery, one low down to house the goose on her nest and the other rounded with a projected curved stone shelf for the water barrel.

Close by the old house, there are later outbuildings as well as traces of rig cultivation and old field dykes.

Mossetter: entrance and neuk-beds in scullery

25* Kirbuster, Farm Museum

AD 1723.

HY 283253. About 3.5 km N of Dounby on the A 986, take the minor road to the NE for 1 km, then take the N fork for rather less than 1 km.

Orkney Islands Council.

Kirbuster Farm Museum: kitchen with fire-back and neuk-bed (Right)

Kirbuster Farm Museum

It is unusual to be able to date an old farm so precisely, and the fact that the date is carved on the marriage lintel above the main door reflects the status of this farm: there was no question here of living under the same roof as the cattle. The walls are unusually high and the house is reasonably well lit by windows, and yet it has undergone remarkably little alteration for a house inhabited until recent times. Its linear range consists of four rooms, of which the kitchen is by far the most interesting, because it was never divided and it retains the free-standing hearth with its stone-built fire-back. The wooden smoke-hole in the roof above has been reconstructed faithfully to the original, and the iron fittings by which cooking pots were suspended above the fire are still fixed to the charred beam above. The peat was kept in a neuk in the wall, the floor well-paved and the fire-back was kept whitewashed. In the south wall, close to the warmth of the fire, there is a beautifully constructed neuk-bed, not housed in a projecting outshot but contained within the thickness of the wall; two large flagstones form the front of the bed, with masonry above, and the neuk would have been snugly lined with wood.

The outbuildings include a barn with a well-preserved corn-drying kiln, a pigsty and a smith's forge, and there is an attractive and sheltered garden.

Tormiston Mill
(Bottom left)

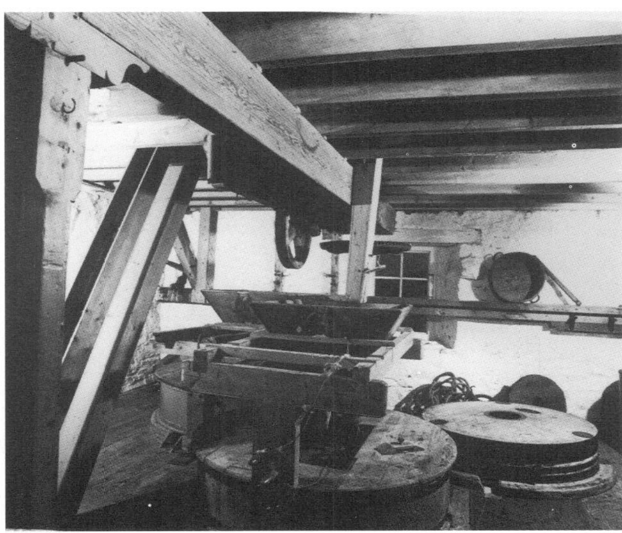

The first floor of Tormiston Mill

26* Tormiston Mill

c AD 1880.

HY 319125. On the A 965 Kirkwall to Stromness road, about 4 km SW of Finstown; signposted, now a visitor centre.

Historic Scotland.

This elegant vertical-wheeled mill has been restored and adapted very successfully as a restaurant and craft shop, the use of natural wood and bare stone retaining an impression internally of the original three-storey mill. The external appearance is excellently preserved with an eight-spoke iron water-wheel, more than 4 m in diameter, with wooden buckets, and an unusual stone aqueduct carrying the water over the wheel. The wheel drove three pairs of millstones on the first floor, and the grain was stored on the top floor after having been dried in a kiln at the far end of the building. With the prehistoric tomb of Maes Howe across the road, this is a very attractive place to linger on a tour of Orkney's mainland monuments.

27* Boardhouse Mill, Birsay

18th-19th centuries AD.

HY 254274. Beside the A 967 from Stromness to Birsay, about 1.5 km SE of Birsay village; signposted.

The three mills surviving at Boardhouse today are themselves the descendants of earlier mills on the burn running from the Loch of Boardhouse to the sea in the Bay of Birsay (see no. 33), and they are fine representatives of a long tradition of milling in what has always been one of the most fertile areas of Orkney. The youngest mill is still working commercially and is particularly well known for its production of beremeal.

The new Barony Corn Mill was the last to be built, and it is a very large three-storey block with a large kiln vent at the apex of the roof, which was completed in 1873; it has three pairs of great millstones, all driven by an iron water-wheel, over 4m in diameter, with wooden buckets. This replaced the Old Barony Corn Mill built in the 18th century, the fabric of which is still in good condition although the water-wheel is incomplete. The third, smaller building is a threshing mill, and it retains its water-wheel intact.

Boardhouse Mill

The name Boardhouse implies that this was part of the lord's home-farm, and it is first recorded in 1634. The Earl's mill is thus likely to have been on the same spot as those that survive, set at the optimum point on the burn for the flow of water from the Loch of Boardhouse.

28 Dounby, Click Mill

Early 19th century AD.

HY 325228. From Dounby in central N mainland, take the B 9057 for almost 4 km; signposted.

Historic Scotland.

This mill is the only surviving example of a horizontal watermill in Orkney, and it has been excellently restored with all its machinery in working order and its flagstone roof intact. It was built around 1823 to replace an older mill in the same place, Millbrig, and it was used throughout most of the rest of that century; it has been necessary to engineer a piped supply of water so that the restored mill can operate for about 8 minutes at a time, because the original water supply was destroyed by quarrying in the burn for stones for road-making in the 1920s.

The building is very small, only about 4.5 m by 2 m, with the entrance in one of the long walls with a small opening or winnowing hole in the opposite wall to create a through draught. There is another unusual feature in the tirl, which has two rows of blades, one set above the other making a total of 12 blades. The mill was said to grind about a bushel of grain per hour (about 250 kilograms).

29 Scar, Windmill, Sanday

Late 18th century AD.

HY 670451. At the terminal of the B 9068 at the NW end of the island.

This is part of a large farm built for the Traill family of Westove, which includes a lectern dovecote and a later steam-powered meal mill. The conical stone windmill base is all that remains of a number of windmills in Sanday in the 19th century. The entrance was at second-floor level.

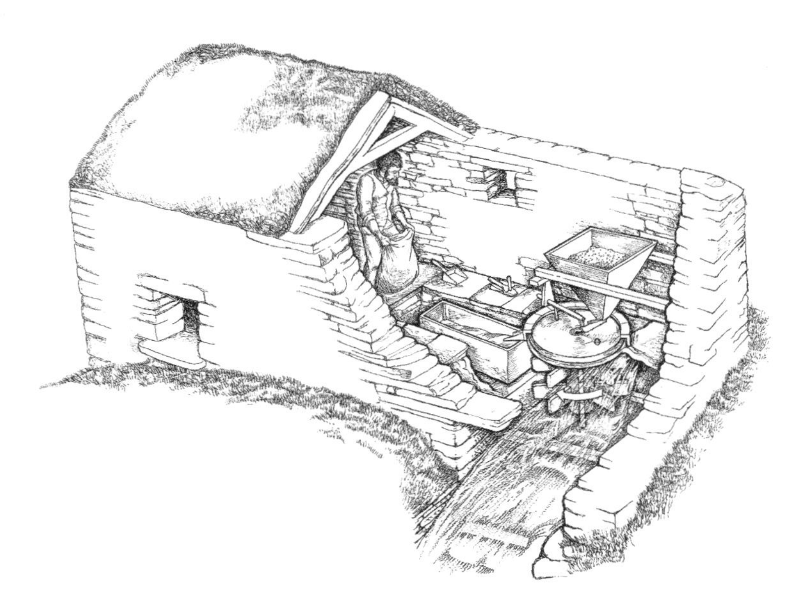

Reconstruction drawing of Dounby Click Mill in operation

The fertile island of Sanday has a number of interesting farm buildings. There was a 'model farm' of the industrialised 19th century at Stove at the south end of the island; the buildings are now ruined but they include an exceptionally large byre for cattle and a red-brick chimney which served a steam-driven mill (HY 608355). At Tresness there is a hexagonal horse-engine house built in the 19th century to power the adjacent threshing-mill (HY 703387), while at Boloquoy may be seen an early 19th-century meal mill with a vertical iron wheel.

30 Peckhole Windmill, North Ronaldsay

Late 18th century AD.

HY 763528. About 0.7 km SE of Holland.

Only the conical stone base of the windmill survives, but its wooden upper parts are shown in the drawing on p.00. This was the last working windmill in Scotland, for it was still in use into the opening years of the 20th century alongside the water-mill built in the early 19th century. The latter building is two-storeyed with a large kiln-vent. Both were replaced by a mill powered by an oil-using engine in 1908.

Scar windmill base

31 North Ronaldsay Dykes

19th century AD and earlier.

HU 7654. The island can be reached by sea or by air from Kirkwall.

The island of North Ronaldsay is famous both for its sheep and for its sheep dyke. The sheep are of a very old native breed and they feed chiefly on seaweed, being confined to the foreshore by a stone dyke, some 1.5 m high, which encircles the entire 19km perimeter of the island. The original 19th century building and continuing maintenance of the dyke represent communal labour by the islanders, and the whole method of sheep husbandry here is an invaluable and almost unique survival of a once widespread communal system of agriculture.

Equally interesting are the two earthen dykes, the Matches Dyke (HY 756546-767544) and the Muckle Gairsty (HY 750534-768521), which run roughly east-west across the island dividing it into three unequal parts. Local legend attributes the dykes to a man who divided the land between his three sons, apparently according to the old udal system of inheritance; whether or not the legend is true, the two dykes are almost certainly territorial boundaries of some sort. Their date is uncertain: they appear on a map published around 1770 but they could well be very much earlier, perhaps prehistoric in origin. There is a particularly well-preserved length of the Muckle Gairsty running south-south-eastwards from Northness in the south-east tip of the island (HY 766527–768522), where it is 4 m wide and almost 2 m high.

5 MEDIEVAL PALACES AND CASTLES

Earl's Palace, Kirkwall

Orkney is fortunate in having a rare well-preserved and indisputable Norse castle of the 12th century on the small island of Wyre (no. 36). There follows a gap in the record of surviving monuments of some 400 years before the main period of building castles and defensive residences begins in the late 16th century, from which have survived some exceptional monuments, culminating in the splendour of the Earl's Palace in Kirkwall. They demonstrate that Orkney shared in the architectural developments taking place on mainland Scotland, in some cases excelling in architectural refinements. A castle that no longer survives is that commemorated in Castle Street, Kirkwall, where Earl Henry Sinclair built a castle in the late 14th century facing St Magnus Cathedral; it was demolished in 1615, though parts of its walls were still in existence until the later 19th century. It was said to have been a particularly strongly built castle.

By the mid 16th century, one very popular design for a stone-built fortification consisted of a main rectangular block with towers attached to two diagonally opposite corners (known to architectural historians as the Z-plan), and there is a good example at Noltland in Orkney (no. 34). The towers not only provided extra accommodation but also added to the defensive potential of the building, allowing more effective coverage of the ground immediately surrounding the building. A great asset was the fact that the entrance could be placed at the angle between a tower and the main block, thus protecting it from several directions by means of small openings for hand-guns.

There seems to have been a strong element of fashion rather than necessity dictating the extent to which castle-design included gun-loops and shot-holes. At this stage in the development of hand-guns, they were in practice almost ludicrously ineffective compared with the longbow or the cross-bow, either of which was much faster to load and more accurate; it has been estimated that the hakbut might fire six or seven one-ounce balls per hour, a sad contrast to the twelve arrows per minute of which a good longbowman was capable. Seen in this light, one can appreciate that the tiers of gun-loops at Noltland Castle were perhaps more effective as a psychological deterrent than as a practical battery.

Noltland Castle by R W Billings

Earl's Palace, Kirkwall

32* Earl's Palace, Kirkwall

AD 1606.

HY 449107. In the centre of the town, close to St Magnus Cathedral.

Historic Scotland.

This building has been described as 'possibly the most mature and accomplished piece of Renaissance architecture left in Scotland', and it is certainly a most attractive monument set amongst trees and well-kept lawns. It was known as the New Wark of the Yards when first built, to distinguish it from the older Bishop's Palace, then known as the Place of the Yards.

As it survives, it is an L-shaped building of two main blocks with a short wing projecting from the north-west corner of the main block, but it seems originally to have conformed to a courtyard plan, though nothing is known of the character of the west and north sides, or if indeed they were ever completed. The ground-floor consists of vaulted storerooms, a vaulted kitchen and a splendidly spacious main stairway leading to the 'state apartments' on the first floor. Traces of a second floor survive very incompletely. The outstanding features of the Palace are the main entrance, the oriel windows and the great fireplace in the hall, but there are many other interesting details.

The main entrance, set at the angle of two wings, is badly weathered but still conveys a strong sense of its former grandeur; there is a Doric element in the deeply moulded half-columns flanking the door, and the capitals were once richly decorated, as were the surrounds of the three panels above the door. The lower panel held an inscription originally, the middle panel displayed the arms of Earl Patrick, and the uppermost panel the royal arms of Scotland, both now barely discernible. Another inscribed panel was set above the corbelled chimney-breast on the adjacent wall. The door itself would have consisted of an outer wooden door and an inner iron gate or yett.

The grand entrance into the Earl's Palace, Kirkwall

The entrance of the great hall on the first-floor is flanked on the left by a small vaulted room, used by the Earl's major-domo, and on the right by a tiny and very attractive room interpreted as an ante-chamber for guests waiting to see the Earl. It has a stone basin in a recess just inside the entrance arch, and its barrel-vaulted ceiling has panels of fine masonry separated by moulded and decorative stone ribs.

The great hall of the Earl's Palace, Kirkwall

The great hall is still a magnificent though roofless chamber, and it is easy to imagine its impact when inhabited, full of people and colour and urgent conversation. It is fully 16.5 m long and 6 m wide, requiring two fireplaces and several fine windows, including a huge window in the south gable with triple round-headed lights. The larger fireplace on the west side of the hall has truly noble proportions: flanked by moulded jambs echoing those of the main entrance, the fireplace is framed by a straight arch some 5 m long, above which there is an arch designed to lessen the strain of the weight of masonry above. The capitals of the jambs on either side are embellished with an earl's coronet and the initials P E O for Patrick, Earl of Orkney. It is recorded that several rooms of the palace were 'curiously painted with Scripture stories', like the Earl's Palace at Birsay (no. 33), and it is likely that the great hall was one of those rooms, perhaps with a painted ceiling.

33 Earl's Palace, Birsay

16th century AD.

HY 248277. In the village of Birsay, close by the A 966.

Historic Scotland.

The striking but gaunt shell of the Earl's Palace still dominates the village and the broad bay of Birsay, and the walls convey a strong sense of its original massive grandeur, but it takes a little imagination to restore an impression of its once magnificent elegance: it was described in 1633 as 'a sumptuous and stately dwelling'. The rooms on the upper floor were attractively decorated with painted ceilings, including biblical scenes with appropriate texts, and they would undoubtedly have been furnished with brightly coloured wall-hangings. The exterior of the building seems always to have been fairly austere, befitting its status as a fortified residence of the Earl of Orkney, but the upper windows of the north and east wings were embellished with carved and pinnacled pediments.

It was built by Robert Stewart, Earl of Orkney, in the latter half of the 16th century as a courtyard house in fashionable Renaissance style, consisting of four wings round a rectangular courtyard with square towers at each corner except that on the north-west. It seems that a decision to modify the original plan was made during the course of a long building programme, because the north wing is awkwardly placed, masking the gable-end of the west wing and very close to the west side of the tower at the north-east corner, as if there was originally to have been only a screen-wall along the north side of the courtyard (and presumably a tower at the north-west corner to match the other three). The fact that the upper-floor windows on the north and east wings match suggest that this change of design took place not long after the completion of the latter wing. In the centre of the courtyard is a circular well. The external walls of the Palace are lined with gun-loops, as were the internal walls lining the courtyard, including one surviving on the west wing which is angled to cover the main entrance into the courtyard from outside. The ground-floor was lit by small horizontal windows as an addition defensive precaution. The entire building was two-storeyed except for the north-east tower which rose an extra storey, but

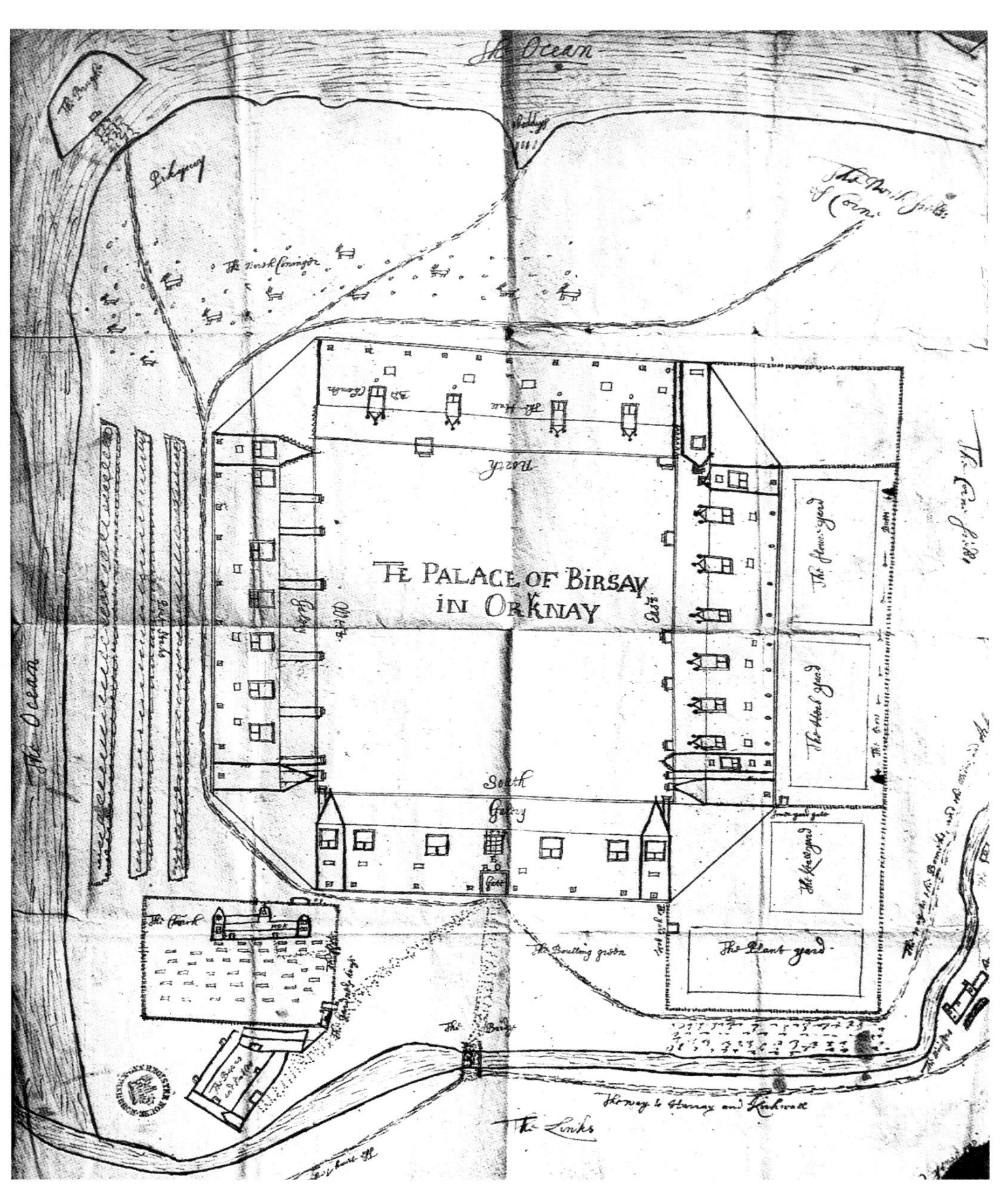

17th-century drawing of the Earl's Palace, Birsay

only the towers, the north wing and part of the west wing survive to any height, for it has been uninhabited since the late 17th century.

There exists a beautifully detailed plan of the Palace, drawn in the 17th century, which shows not only the missing upper storeys but the main entrance with the initials R E O for Robert Earl of Orkney and the date 1574 above what may be either a window or, more probably, an armorial panel. It also shows the immediate setting of the Palace: the pathway leading out to Skipi Geo to the north where boats were landed, huge peat-stacks on the west between the Palace and the shore of the bay and a range of walled enclosures down the east side of the building, including a 'Floure Yard' or flower garden and a 'Herbe Yard'. The 'Bow Butts' ran the length of these two gardens, so that the ladies could admire the archers at their targets practice, and there was a bowling green in front of the Palace.

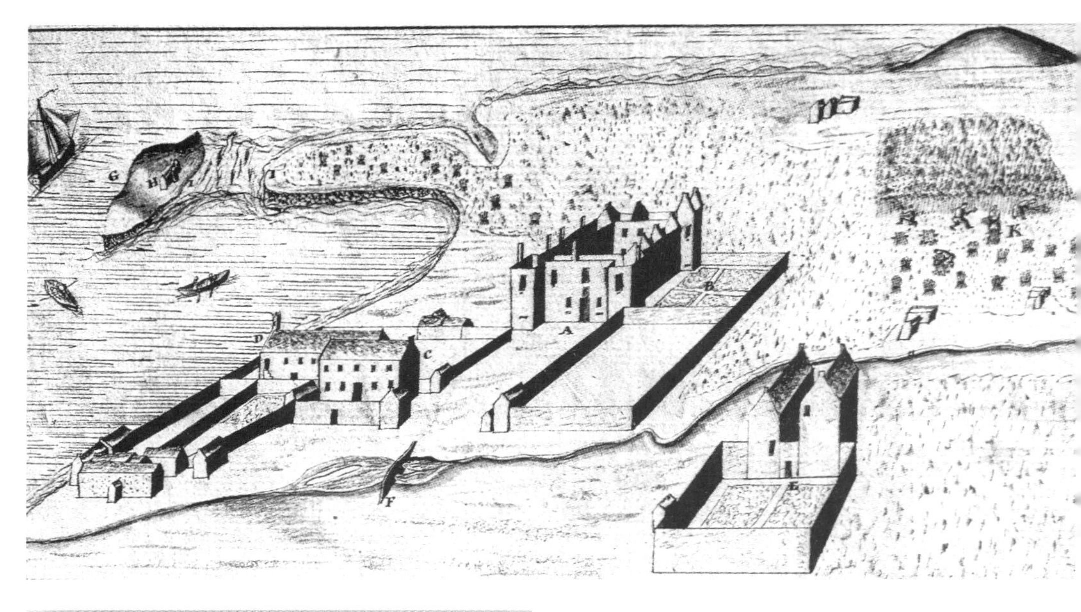

18th-century drawing of the Earl's Palace, Birsay

Earl's Palace, Birsay

The drawing also shows the church and churchyard (no. 38) close to the south-west corner of the Palace, and a courtyard range south of the churchyard. It is possible that this represents the old episcopal palace, by now converted into barns and stables for the Earl.

The bridge over the Barony burn to the south of the Earl's Palace has a longer history than is immediately apparent. It is a stone-built bridge with two arches and, although the upper part was reconstructed in 1872, the lower part may well be medieval. A two-span bridge is certainly shown on an 18th-century drawing and a bridge on the same spot on the 17th-century drawing already mentioned. A bridge over the burn was vital to access from Kirkwall and elsewhere on mainland, unlike the modern approach from the north-east of the Palace.

34* Noltland Castle, Westray

16th century AD.

HY 429486. Close to the road, 800 m W of Pierowall.

Historic Scotland.

The siting of this most impressive castle emphasises the importance in former times of the natural harbour at Pierowall, and the height of the parapet provides an extensive view of the northern isles of Orkney. Most of the building uses the local grey flagstone but the finer stonework consists of red sandstone which was probably imported from Eday, a short voyage to the south-east of Westray. Though roofless, the castle survives in good condition, despite the fact that it was never completed, and it is an excellent example of a 16th-century Z-plan design with a central block and two towers. Most remarkable of all is the number of gun-loops, no fewer than 71 arranged in tiers, making it an unusually fearsome building, which was probably their prime purpose.

The main rectangular block measures 26.5m by 11m and, though incomplete, was designed to have three upper storeys, with square towers at its south-west and north-east angles; the south-west tower is slightly bigger at 9 m square than the north-east tower, presumably because it enclosed not only the

Noltland Castle

Noltland Castle, main stair

entrance but the main stairway. Although initially the castle looks very severe, there are decorative details. The lower string-course on the south-west tower is moulded and bears traces of carving, while the moulded panel above the doorway would originally have held a carved armorial panel, and at the well-head there were once turrets and a parapet walk supported by the decorative projecting corbels that still survive. The gables were stepped. The inside of the castle, at least on the upper floors, must have been quite elegant to judge from the proportions of the main hall and the spacious design of the stairway, one of the finest of its period in Scotland, leading from the entrance up to the hall. The central newel of the stair is finished at the top with a great carved stone terminal.

Noltland Castle, carved newel above main stair

The hall may also be reached by a back stair from the kitchen below to a small servery where finishing touches might be added to meals about to be served in the great hall (a convenience not matched by conditions in the kitchen, which must have been very dark and stuffy). The basement was originally divided into two levels by a wooden floor creating storerooms between the kitchen and the vaulted stone ceiling that supports the hall and chamber on the first floor. The passion for gun-loops, which are such a feature of the castle, even extended to placing two in the wall at the back of the huge fireplace in the kitchen. It is worth examining the gun-loops in the basement, because many have slots designed to hold wooden mountings for the guns.

On the first floor were not only the hall and the laird's private apartments but also, beside the stair in the south-west tower, a small chamber that seems to have acted as a strong-room, because there are lockers with secret compartments built into the sills of the two windows.

The courtyard on the south side of the castle with its arched gateway and foundations of domestic buildings is a later addition, described in an 18th-century document as a `garden'. The castle itself was built sometime between 1560 and 1574 by Gilbert Balfour, a Scot from Fife with a particularly ruthless personal history, who had acquired through marriage lands in Westray in 1560. Despite the fact that Noltland was never properly finished, it was used for at least two centuries both as a military stronghold and as a residence.

35* Bishop's Palace, Kirkwall

12th-17th centuries AD.

HY 449108. At the corner of Palace Road and Watergate.

Historic Scotland.

The Bishop's Palace is Kirkwall's oldest surviving secular building, although there has been some controversy in academic circles over just how old its foundations may be. Most of the building as it survives today dates from the time of Bishop Robert Reid in the mid 16th century, but it has been argued that the lowest part of the main block

Bishop's Palace, Kirkwall, interior with St Magnus Cathedral beyond

includes the remains of an earlier episcopal residence, perhaps that of Bishop William, under whom the seat of the bishopric was transferred from Birsay to Kirkwall to accompany the building of the new Cathedral in the mid 12th century. This early palace would have been a rectangular hall-house, with a ground-floor given over to storage and workrooms and a great hall on the first floor. It was here that the Norwegian King Haakon died in 1263 after his crushing defeat in western Scotland at the Battle of Largs. Nothing remains of this hall-house above its basal courses, and even those are overshadowed by the rise in ground-level outside.

Bishop Reid's reconstruction of the building in the mid 16th century retained the basic design of first-floor hall and ground-floor storage, but he added not only another storey plus attic but also the great round tower at the north-west corner, which contained five storeys (including his own personal apartments) and an attic. The building thus became considerably more grand and ample in its accommodation. The weathered statue carved in white stone and set off by the red sandstone of its niche in the outer wall of the tower has been variously identified as St Olaf, Bishop Reid and Earl Rognvald Kali Kolsson who ruled Orkney from 1136 to 1158 (this statue is a cast and the original is in Tankerness House Museum). The identification of Earl Rognvald hinges on the object at his feet, which appears to be a lyre, for the Earl was famous as a musician.

The details of the arrangement of rooms on the upper floors of the main block are uncertain, as only the shell of the building survives, and its analysis is further hampered by the fact that it was again modified, probably around 1600 by Earl Patrick as part of his own palace complex. Early drawings and accounts of the building make clear that there were, until about 1800, two square towers, apparently free-standing, close to its north-east end, nothing of which can now be seen.

The round tower is in itself an interesting structure and must originally have been a very imposing addition to the house. Although round externally, the rooms inside were approximately square, and the spiral stair rises within the thickness of the wall. The parapet is supported by decorative corbelling and the parapet-walk was originally roofed over, a very unusual design. The tower had a square cap-house rising above the level of the parapet-roof, with a small square room inside.

A splendid view can be had from the top of the tower over St Magnus Cathedral.

36 Cubbie Roo's Castle, Wyre

12th century AD.

HY 441262. On the NW side of the island, overlooking Wyre Sound; a walk of some 1.5 km from the jetty, by ferry from Tingwall.

Historic Scotland.

'At that time there was a very able man named Kolbein Hruga farming on Wyre in Orkney. He had a fine stone fort built there, a really solid stronghold' - so records *Orkneyinga Saga* of events

Bishop's Palace, Kirkwall: Bishop Reid's tower (Left)

around 1150, and the same castle is described as a difficult place to attack in 1231 in *Haakonar Saga*. Although in the past there has been controversy over its date, the small stone castle surviving on Wyre is now generally accepted as that built in the 12th century by Kolbein, whose Norse nickname would have been Kobbie or Kubbie, hence the modern name, Cubbie Roo (Hruga has become Roo). It is thus one of the earliest stone-built castles in Scotland and certainly the best preserved, having been excavated in the late 1920s and later consolidated.

In its original design, the castle consisted of an almost square keep, about 8 m across with mortared walls almost 2 m thick, surrounded at a distance of about 8 m by outer defences: a stone wall with an outer ditch and bank. Only the ground floor of the keep survives complete, but it must have risen at least two more floors to have achieve a good view over the island and the surrounding seaways; the narrow projecting ledge that supported the timber first floor can be seen on the inner face of the north wall. Access to the upper floors would have been by internal wooden ladders, and the sole entrance to the keep was at first-floor level, again reached by a retractable wooden ladder (although this doorway no longer survives, it was recorded in the late 17th century). The ground floor was probably used for storing supplies, as were those of later tower-houses, and a rectangular tank cut into the solid rock was presumably used either to store drinking water or to keep a living supply of fish. It is doubtful that the keep was a permanent residence; it seems more likely that it was used as a refuge in times of trouble, for its size is quite unsuited to the establishment of an important Norse family, and the name of the adjacent modern farm, the Bu of Wyre, suggests the existence of a separate Norse farmstead with its great hall and outbuildings. The church belonging to the 12th-century estate still survives (no. 42).

The enclosing defences survive only to the west, north and east of the keep, for elsewhere they have been obliterated by later building. The excavations identified at least five phases of subsequent building and modification around the keep, some of which may be as early as the 13th century, and the entire complex is testimony to the success of the original design. Neither of the other two fortifications mentioned in *Orkneyinga Saga*, at Cairston near Stromness and on the island of Damsay, survived so long.

Interior of Cubbie Roo's Castle

6 CHURCHES AND GRAVE STONES

The church and round tower of St Magnus, Egilsay, from the air

The Reformation led to no major changes to the medieval churches of Orkney, for their simple layout was easily adapted to congregational worship. At Pierowall (no. 37) the old chancel was replaced by a laird's aisle and the nave was widened, but in most cases there was no re-building, and even the round church at Orphir survived until the latter part of the 18th century, its form perhaps well suited, if unorthodox, to the new ideas. Natural wastage coupled with sheer old age brought about the abandonment of many churches, and many were demolished in the late 18th century when new parish churches were built.

The new churches of the 17th and 18th centuries were simple rectangular buildings, sometimes with a laird's aisle projecting from one long side. A fine series of contemporary tombstones may be seen in St Magnus Cathedral (no. 40), including 17th-century examples with particularly excellent lettering rivalled by two at Pierowall (no. 37).

Medieval churches

Orkney is fortunate in the number and variety of its surviving medieval churches, even though St Magnus Cathedral in Kirkwall stands in a class of its own, there being no other building of remotely comparable architectural quality or elaboration. There are several Romanesque churches of the 12th century which, though roofless, have well-preserved walls and architectural details. These are mostly characterised by rectangular naves and square-ended chancels, with round-arched doorways and windows, but there is one survivor of a group of churches with tall round towers: St Magnus Church on Egilsay (no. 41). Formerly there were similar churches, known as `steeple-kirks', at Stenness and Deerness in Orkney (the latter with twin towers) and at Tingwall, Ireland and Papil in Shetland, most of which were demolished in the late 18th century. These round towers are part of an architectural tradition that developed round the North Sea in the 12th century.

At two Orcadian churches, Brough of Birsay (no. 49) and Eynhallow (no. 44), it is possible that there was once a square tower at the west end, reduced to its foundations at the first site and to a porch at the second. If these were towers, they might demonstrate continuing influence from Northumbria, and at Birsay there is certainly Norwegian church design reflected in the circular altar recesses on either side at the eastern end of the nave.

As they survive today, these small medieval churches give an impression of bleak austerity, but their plain architecture would have been countered by colour and lightness in their interiors, and in some cases there was architectural embellishment in the form of stone-carving, since removed (eg Eynhallow, no. 44) or lost. Traces of plastering indicate that the rubble walls were smooth and light in colour (and may have been painted), and the stone dressings around doorways and windows sometimes included red sandstone. Internal furnishings might include woven wall-hangings, carved and painted wooden fittings and silver chalices and candlesticks. Seating, if any, would be narrow stone or wooden benches set along the walls, such as still survive in stone on the Brough of Birsay (no. 49). Roofing would be flagstones, turf or thatch on a wooden frame.

A number of churches bear the name `cross-kirk', but it implies dedication to the Holy Rude rather than architectural design as a cruciform church, although a few cruciform churches seem to have existed, for example at Birsay (demolished).

Orphir church (no. 39) is the only surviving Scottish example of a design briefly fashionable in medieval western Europe; modelled on the Church of the Holy Sepulchre in Jerusalem, such round churches were built during the period of the Crusades to the Holy Land by returning crusaders or `Jerusalem farers' as they are termed in runes inscribed inside Maes Howe (no. 72). Comparable round churches may be seen, for example, in Denmark today, mostly incorporated into larger churches. The church at Orphir was part of an earl's estate, built close to the great hall, and other

Part of the nave and the apse survive of the round church at Orphir

12th-century churches have proved to be part of great Norse family estates: the church on Wyre was built close to both the domestic farmstead and the castle (no. 36), while in Westray excavations have revealed a high status late Norse settlement at Tuquoy close to the contemporary Cross Kirk or Westside church (no. 43).

Although the documentary and archaeological evidence is controversial, the buildings on Eynhallow (no. 44) may well have been a medieval monastery. To judge by known monasteries in other Atlantic Norse colonies, such sites would look far more like normal farms than like the great monasteries of southern Scotland and England and would be correspondingly more difficult to recognise. The Brough of Deerness (no. 48) was for a long time thought to be the site of a medieval monastery, but excavations have suggested that, although there is a small rectangular chapel of Norse date, the surrounding houses are likely to be of secular rather than ecclesiastical nature, a situation parallel to that on the Brough of Birsay (no. 49).

The influences from eastern Scotland and north-east England on the architecture of St Magnus Cathedral are unmistakeable, and the same influences gave rise to an equally distinctive fashion in gravestones: the hogback monument. This is a recumbent stone placed lengthwise over the grave, shaped and carved to imitate a house with a curved roof-ridge, and it is a style that was invented in the 10th century by Scandinavian settlers in North Yorkshire. In Scotland, hogbacks are mostly found in central and eastern areas, no further north than Angus, and the group in the Northern Isles must represent direct contact by sea with these areas further south.

Few monuments are still in their original positions, such as that in the churchyard of St Boniface on Papa Westray, Orkney (no. 46), and they are late examples dating to the 12th century by which time the roof-ridge had flattened and lost its characteristic curved hogback shape. Examples of true hogbacks of 11th-century date may be seen in Tankerness House Museum in Kirkwall, found originally in St Olaf's Churchyard and beneath the chancel of St Magnus Cathedral.

The 17th-century burial aisle of the Moodies of Melsetter at Osmondwall in Walls; built into one gable are two heraldic panels and part of a 16th-century graveslab

Lady Kirk, Pierowall

17th-century graveslabs at Lady Kirk, Pierowall (Left)

37 Lady Kirk, Pierowall, Westray

17th century AD.

HY 439488. In Pierowall on the shore of the bay, 1 km SW of the pier.

Historic Scotland.

There are traces of the medieval fabric in the walls of this church, but most of the visible structure was built in the late 17th century, and the date of 1674 is carved on the south skewput (the lowest stone at eaves level) of the east gable. The nave was re-aligned, somewhat wider than before, and the chancel was replaced by a laird's aisle, the whole structure distinctly canted. The west gable is topped by a 'birdcage' bellcote with a ball finial. Within the laird's aisle are two 17th-century tombstones with exceptionally fine lettering, one of which has the emblems of mortality carved in high relief and an effective chequered margin.

St Magnus Church, Birsay

The re-used window with its inscribed sill

38 St Magnus Church, Birsay

AD 1664 and 1760.

HY 247277. Beside the A 966 in the village of Birsay.

This long rectangular church is more interesting than it first appears. It was built in 1664 and extended a century later, and a small porch was added during alterations in 1867. The bellcote at the west end may date to the original building, but there are also features surviving from structures earlier than the 1664 church. These include a narrow round-arched doorway (blocked) and a small lancet window in the north wall, and another lancet window in the south wall, all of which were probably part of an earlier church on the site. The south window has as its sill a stone with an inscription. This was once part of a lintel and it reads SBELLUS; another fragment of the same lintel is built into a nearby cottage, and together they read MONSBELLUS. This was the name used in the 16th century for the Bishop of Orkney's residence at Birsay, and it is likely that this lintel once embellished the episcopal palace.

Inside the church are a small late medieval font and a 17th-century graveslab, while in the churchyard may be seen several 18th-century graveslabs. Excavation close to the church wall has revealed foundations likely to belong to the pre-1664 church, which is recorded as having been cruciform in plan.

39 St Nicholas Church, Orphir

Early 12th century AD.

HY 334044. On the A 964 about 14.5 km from Kirkwall, take the minor road to Orphir; signposted.

Historic Scotland; Orkney Islands Council Visitor Centre.

To visit Orphir is to be transported back into saga-times, for despite their fragmentary state the remains of these buildings neatly fit one of the few circumstantial descriptions in *Orkneyinga Saga*.

'There was a great drinking-hall at Orphir, with a door in the south wall near the eastern gable, and in front of the hall, just a few paces down from it, stood a fine church. On the left as you came into the hall was a large stone slab, with a lot of big ale vats behind it, and opposite the door was the living-room.'

In the early 12th century, Orphir was the seat of Earl Haakon Paulsson, who was responsible for the murder of Earl Magnus on Egilsay c 1117 but managed himself to die peacefully in his bed five years later. In between those events, he made a pilgrimage to Rome and to Jerusalem where, we are told, 'he visited the holy places and bathed in the River Jordan'. One of the places that he would have visited was the Church of the Holy Sepulchre, and this must have been the impetus to building a similar round church on his own estate at Orphir.

Aerial view of St Nicholas Church and the Earl's Bu, Orphir

Only a third of the church survives but the rest of its plan is marked out on the ground: a precisely circular nave, 6.1 m in internal diameter, into which there would presumably have been an entrance at the west with a semicircular apse on the east.

The church was complete until 1757, when it was largely demolished and its masonry used to build a new parish church alongside; ironically, the latter has now been demolished to reveal as much as possible of the earlier church. The apse is still intact with its half-barrel ceiling and internal plastering and a rounded-headed window above the seating for the altar, and early accounts of the nave describe its domed roof with a central hole to provide light.

A few metres away, or a few paces as the saga-writer put it, are the excavated walls of a large building, most probably the Earl's hall. Late Norse artefacts have been found in the vicinity, but more excavation is needed to establish the layout and extent of this important site. Beside the road have been excavated, beneath a late Norse midden, the remains of a horizontal corn-mill which evidently served the Orphir estate at an earlier period.

The superstructure of the mill has gone, but visible are the underhouse that contained the horizontal paddles, the lade that supplied the water to drive the machinery and the tail-race that took the water away.

St Magnus Cathedral and the Bishop's Palace drawn by R W Billings in the late 19th century

40* St Magnus Cathedral, Kirkwall

12th-15th centuries AD.

HY 449108. In the centre of the town.

The history of this remarkable cathedral goes back beyond the year in which its long programme of building began, 1136 or 1137, to the year in which died the man to whom it was dedicated: Earl Magnus, who was murdered on Egilsay c 1116. His body was taken to Christ Church at Birsay and became a focus of pilgrimage. *Orkneyinga Saga* relates that 'a bright heavenly light was often seen over Magnus' grave' and that people were cured of illnesses by praying at his graveside. At first the church in Orkney was highly sceptical of the new cult growing up around Magnus, but eventually he was accepted as a saint and his bones became holy relics. Some time later, Bishop William was persuaded to transfer the relics to the church in Kirkwall, presumably St Olaf's Church (no. 45).

According to the saga, the impetus to build a new cathedral at Kirkwall came not from within the church but as a vow made by Earl Rognvald, then seeking control of the earldom: if he succeeded, he would build 'a stone minster at Kirkwall more magnificent than any in Orkney', which would be dedicated to St Magnus and would hold his relics. The episcopal seat was also to be in Kirkwall, and it has been suggested that Rognvald's vow reflects not only the medieval belief in the efficacy of saintly relics but also a shrewd political move on the part of the Orcadian Church, promising support for Rognvald in return for a fine cathedral and a new and more powerful centre for the bishopric. Rognvald succeeded in taking over the earldom and work began on building the Cathedral of St Magnus.

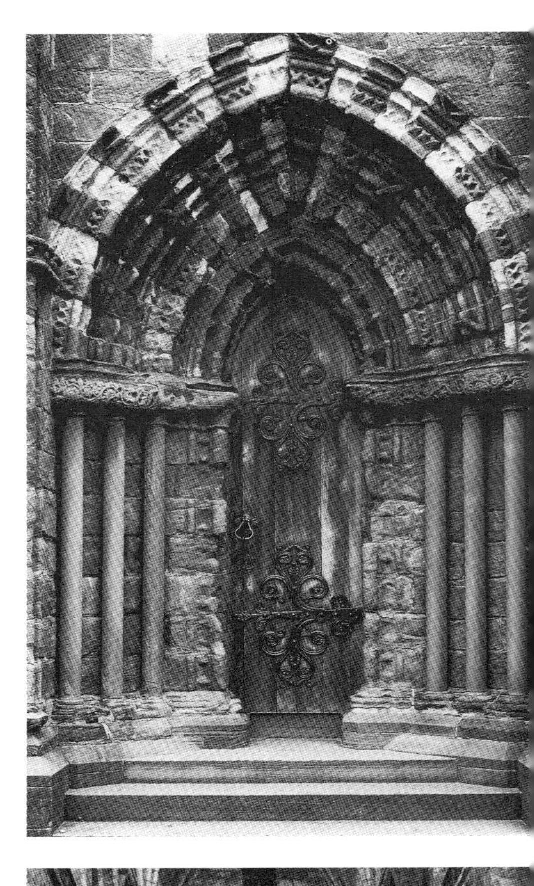

St Magnus Cathedral: door in west front (Right)

Its completion was to take far longer than anyone can have envisaged at the start, but its final splendour was well worth the delay. Indeed it was a magnificent structure at all intervening stages of the work, for the earliest part to be built was the choir, completed probably around 1142, which has been described as 'the finest Romanesque work north of Durham'. Comparison with both Durham and Dunfermline suggests that either Englishmen or Scotsmen were responsible for the design and execution of St Magnus Cathedral, a practice familiar from Norway itself at this period, when foreign expertise was often sought to build the great churches.

It appears that the foundations were laid at the start for the whole building, and work on the superstructure began at the east end of what was designed to be a cruciform Romanesque church with aisled choir and nave, projecting transepts and an apse at the east end. As work progressed, this design was modified and enlarged, and its style changed according to the fashion of the time. Compare the piers of the nave, for instance: at the east end, the first pier on the north side and the first two on the south are in early 12th-century

The nave of St Magnus Cathedral (Right)

Romanesque style with multicubical capitals and chamfered bases, whereas the next five piers on the north and four on the south are in late 12th-century Transitional style with moulded capitals and bases. In the 13th century the building was enlarged by removing the apse at the east end and extending the aisled choir eastwards for another three bays. The three doorways at the west end of the cathedral were built at this time, enriched with carved decoration similar to that used in the choir, each with shafted jambs and pointed arches. Notice the use of alternate red and white stone in the arches, for this is one of the major and very pleasing decorative devices used inside the church as well, for instance as horizontal banding on the east wall of the south transept.

Prior to whitewashing in the 19th century, the interior was even more colourful, for it was painted with formal designs in red and black; unfortunately little traces of this survives, for both the whitewash and most of the underlying paintwork were removed in the late 19th century. Although the structure of the cathedral was completed in the 15th century, there have inevitably been some changes since then, the most radical external change being the replacement of the original spire, destroyed by lightning in 1671, by a pyramidal wooden roof.

There is a fine series of medieval and later tombstones in the Cathedral, including the Paplay tomb, a 14th-century arched tomb recessed into the wall of the south aisle of the nave. Other sculptures include early 16th-century effigies of St Magnus and the Norwegian King Olaf, as well as the burgh mercat cross. Three famous men of the 12th century were buried in the new minster: Bishop William, Earl Rognvald and, eventually, St Magnus himself. The bones of Bishop William were discovered in 1848 in a tomb in the choir - he had apparently been moved from the original choir into the newly extended east end in the 13th century. Both having been canonised, the bones of St Rognvald and St Magnus would have been kept in resplendent caskets or reliquaries in the choir, until they were hidden for safety at the time of the Reformation. In each of the rectangular piers separating the 12th-century choir from its 13th-century extension, there is a cavity at a height of about 2.7 m; that in the north pier was discovered in 1848 and in it was a wooden box containing the loose bones of an incomplete male skeleton believed to be that of Rognvald, and a similar discovery in 1919 in the south pier contained the bones of St Magnus. The saga account of Magnus' death makes it clear that he died of a great blow on the head, and the skull in the casket showed unmistakeable signs of such a blow.

41 St Magnus Church, Egilsay

12th century AD.

HY 466303. The church stands on a knoll some 700 m E of the pier of the W side of the island; ferry from Tingwall.

Historic Scotland.

This is one of the finest of the early churches in the Northern Isles, dedicated to the earl who was murdered on the island c 1116, Magnus Erlendsson. It is thought to have replaced an earlier church in which Earl Magnus prayed before his death, and the spot where tradition believes the fatal blow to have been struck (HY 470300) is marked by a

The roof over the nave in St Magnus Cathedral (Left)

monument set up in 1937, the octocentenary of the foundation of St Magnus Cathedral.

Although roofless, the church is otherwise virtually complete, and its elegant tower still dominates the island. Built in Romanesque style, probably in the second quarter of the 12th century, it consists of a rectangular nave with a square-ended chancel at its east end and a round tower at its west end; the doorways and the original windows have rounded arches, and the chancel has a barrel-vaulted roof. There was an upper floor to the chancel, where the priest could lodge overnight. The north door to the nave and all the windows (including two later lintelled windows) have been blocked up since the church went out of use in the early 19th century, but it is possible to see the bar-hole on the east side of the south door to the nave, which held the bar to close the wooden door from the inside in times of trouble. At such times the tower could become an invaluable sanctuary, for it could be entered only from within the church; as well as the ground-floor door, one on the first-floor gave access to an upper gallery in the nave, from which the priest's lodging over the chancel could also be reached. The tower survives to a height of 14.9 m but it was originally higher, perhaps almost 20 m high with four or five storeys, reached one from another by wooden ladders. The arrangement of windows in the tower is very ingenious: on the ground floor the window faces south, on the first floor it faces west, on the second east and on the third there are four windows, one to each quarter of the compass. A sketch of the church in 1822 shows flagstone roofs, including a conical roof to the tower, and the gables still retain their crowsteps.

St Magnus Church, Egilsay, drawing

Egilsay Church. From South-West.

The Norse family chapel of St Mary's in Wyre

42 St Mary's Chapel, Wyre

12th century AD.

HY 443262. On the NW side of the island close to Cubbie Roo's Castle (no. 36); a walk of some 1.5 km from the jetty, by ferry from Tingwall.

Historic Scotland.

This typical Romanesque chapel was built in the 12th century to serve the Christian Norse family whose hall or Bu is remembered in the name of the modern farm, the Bu of Wyre, and for whom Cubbie Roo's Castle (no. 36) was built. Although roofless, it is in good repair not only because it is in State care but also because it was partially restored in the late 19th century by General Traill Burroughs of Trumland House on Rousay.

Consisting of a rectangular nave and a square chancel, both chancel and nave are entered through semicircular arches, and traces of the original plaster may be seen on the inside walls and, beneath modern harling, on the exterior. A single window survives high in the south wall of the nave and another in the chancel.

43 Crosskirk, Westside, Westray

12th century AD.

HY 455432. Signposted from the B 9067 at the SW tip of the island.

Historic Scotland.

Originally this church consisted of a small rectangular nave with a barrel-vaulted chancel at the east end, but subsequently the nave was extended westwards, more than doubling its capacity. About 70 m to the west, coastal erosion has revealed and excavation has confirmed the existence of an extensive late Norse settlement, and the church may well have served this estate.

44 Eynhallow Church, Eynhallow

12th century AD.

HY 359288. In the S part of the island; enquire of the Orkney Tourist Office about means of reaching the island.

Historic Scotland.

The original identity of this most interesting group of buildings was entirely unsuspected until the mid 19th century. They had been in domestic use as

Eynhallow Church: the doorways show a remarkable variety of lintels

houses since the 16th century until, in 1851, an epidemic of fever led to their evacuation; in order to make the buildings uninhabitable, the roofs were removed and in the process it was realised that part of the complex was an old church. The site was not properly cleared of debris until 1897, when the celebrated architect of Melsetter (no. 12), Professor W R Lethaby, was there to examine and report on the structure.

The name Eynhallow means Holy Isle from Old Norse, *Eyin Helga*, which suggests that there may have been a small Celtic monastery here even before the 12th-century church was built. Its monastic status at the latter period is implied by the story in *Orkneyinga Saga* (chap. 97) of the kidnapping of Olaf, the son of Svein Asleifarson of Gairsay and foster-son of Kolbein Hruga of Wyre; the kidnappers knew where to find Olaf on Eynhallow, and it is most likely that the boy was there to be educated in the monastery.

The church was built to a relatively sophisticated design: a rectangular nave opens at the east end into a rectangular chancel and at the west end into a substantial square porch (it is even possible that the latter represents the lower part of a tower). Although the walls both of the church and the adjacent buildings survive to roof-level, it is very difficult to analyse the architectural sequences present, because of additions and modifications relating to the domestic use of the site from the 16th century onwards, though the latter are interesting in themselves. The archaic, even primitive, character of various of the doorways and archways of the church is unmistakeable and somewhat at variance with the grand layout. The west and north doorways into the porch are original and very narrow (0.46 m): the triangular arch of the west door is formed by two inclined slabs, while the round arch of the north door is cut into a single block of red freestone with a crude moulding on its external face. Entry into the nave is through a semi-circular arch of split slabs, while the arch between nave and chancel is a most ingenious rendering of the pointed arch that became fashionable in the 12th century. The springers and keystone are triangular blocks carved out of red freestone, allowing the rest of the arch to consist of the usual split slabs, a most economical way to achieve a pointed arch without mortar and with the minimum of dressed stone.

45 St Olaf's Church, Doorway, Kirkwall

11th century AD.

In St Olaf's Wynd off Bridge Street.

All that survives of this church, the first built in Kirkwall and the kirk of the place-name, is a weathered but still impressive doorway now set into a wall in St Olaf's Wynd. Carved of sandstone blocks, it has a heavily ornate moulding. It is thought that the church may may been built by Earl Rognvald Brusason, who is recorded in *Orkneyinga Saga* as having a residence in Kirkwall in the mid 11th century and who was Olaf's foster-son. It was to this church that the relics of St Magnus were brought from Birsay, prior to the building of St Magnus Cathedral. A hogback tombstone of 11th-century date was found in the churchyard (now in Tankerness House Museum).

The later history of the church is uncertain, until the mid 16th century when Bishop Robert Reid is recorded as having reconstructed St Olaf's Church. The carved sandstone aumbry preserved in the 19th-century St Olaf's Church is likely to belong to Bishop Reid's reconstruction of the older church. Although St Olaf's was eclipsed by the creation of St Magnus Cathedral, it clearly retained a role in the life of Kirkwall for several centuries.

St Boniface Church in Papa Westray has been restored

The moulded doorway of St Olaf's Church (Top left)

46 St Boniface Church and Hogback Tombstone, Papa Westray

12th century AD.

HY 488527. On the W side of the island, approached by a track leading W from the road between Holland and North Hill.

Orkney Islands Council.

There is a long history of activity on this site from Iron-age times onwards into the 20th century. Initially there was a domestic settlement established around the 6th century BC and including a massive roundhouse, and this settlement appears to have continued through the first thousand years AD. Excavation in 1990 caught the last vestiges of the roundhouse before coastal erosion claimed it, but the site had been known, and indeed visible in the cliff-section, for more than a century. The settlement was clearly of some importance, probably the major farm in the island in its time, and it was the obvious place to choose when a Christian monastery was established in the 8th century. Folk memory of this monastic site lingers on in the name Munkerhoose, monks' house.

Nothing structural has been found of this early monastery, but the presence of two cross-slabs and part of a stone-built shrine datable to the 8th century are tangible evidence of its existence. There is also documentary and place-name evidence, especially the name coined for the island by the incoming Vikings, for *papae* was their term for priests and monks.

The early church appears to have continued in use throughout Norse times. In the 12th century, the island was part of a large estate based on North Ronaldsay, and a new church was built, which was dedicated to St Boniface and is the core of the church that survives today. It consisted of a small nave and chancel, but the former was extended westwards in 1700 to accommodate an internal gallery served by an external stair, and the chancel was demolished at some unknown date. Its position was used for the burial enclosure of the Traill family, who lived at Holland.

The importance of the church here in Norse times is reflected by the fact recorded in *Orkneyinga Saga* that an earl was buried in Papa Westray in the mid 11th century (chap.30). A tombstone of Norse type is still to be seen in the churchyard, but its style dates it to the following century. This is a late version of the hogback, and it lies in an east-west direction, accompanied by a small upright headstone. It is carved from a block of red sandstone, 1.55 m long, with a deep groove running along its flat ridge and three rows of tegulae (roof-tiles) carved along each side. It is one of the few examples in Scotland of a hogback which appears still to be in its original position.

Though weathered, the carved roof-tiles can still be seen on the hogback in St Boniface churchyard

47 Skaill, Hogback Tombstone, Deerness

Late 11th - early 12th century AD.

HY 588063. At the termination of the A690 from Kirkwall to Deerness, take the B 9050 to Skaill. The stone is inside the Session House attached to the modern church.

This is a well-preserved hogback of red sandstone, 1.73 m long, with four rows of tegulae or roof-tiles carved along either side, the tiles increasing in size towards the base. It was found in the north-east corner of the churchyard, lying east-north-east/west-south-west, and originally belonged to an earlier church on the site. A fine church wit twin towers, comparable to the single-towere St Magnus on Egilsay (no. 41), is known to hav existed here and an Early Christian ancestry for th site is indicated by the recent find from nearb excavations of a fragment of a cross-incised grave marker. These excavations have uncovered a Nors farm and an earlier Pictish settlement, and it clear that Skaill has a long history of Dark Ag Viking and medieval settlement against which it hogback monument may be set. In the 11th centur Skaill was the Orkney home of Thorkell, foste father to Earl Thorfinn, and it was undoubtedly Christian Norse household.

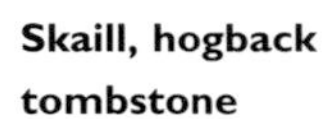

Skaill, hogback tombstone

7 VIKINGS, PICTS AND BROCH-BUILDERS

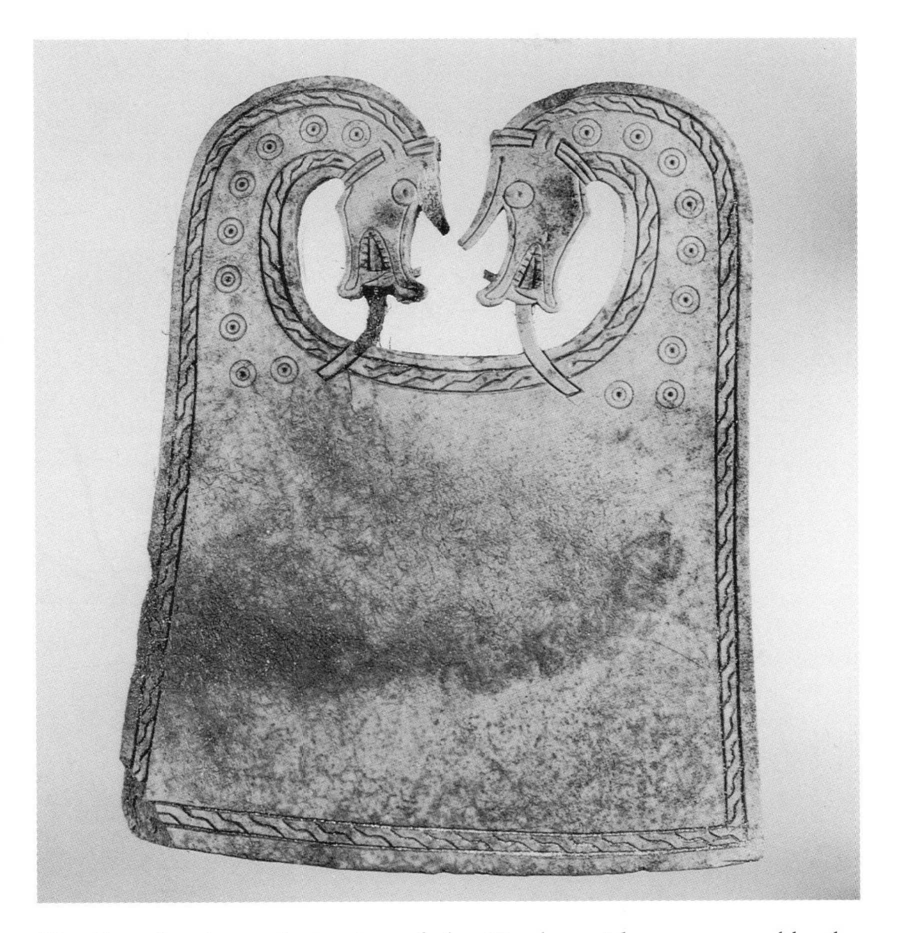

This superb whalebone plaque was found in the Scar boat-burial

The Scandinavian colonisation of the Northern Isles was arguably the single most formative event in their history since the initial human settlement of these islands, and yet there are remarkably few proven Viking-age monuments to be seen on the ground. The situation is even more noticeable elsewhere in Scotland and in the British Isles in general, where there are greater problems of locating sites of this period, let alone of preserving them - with the notable exception, of course, of the great trading centres of York and Dublin. In Orkney, many sites are discovered through coastal erosion (with consequent problems for their preservation), and *Orkneyinga Saga* with its named farms and locations is an invaluable tool. Many more settlements and graves have been located and even excavated than remain as visible monuments, and there is a strong case for rectifying the balance by preserving and opening to the public the complex at Westness on Rousay in Orkney (HY 375294); here there are not only the domestic buildings of a settlement but, on the shore, a contemporary boat-naust in which the family longship could be sheltered over the winter, and the family cemetery in which an amazing variety of graves has been found, including a burial in a real timber boat and a skeuomorphic boat-grave built in stone, together with rich gravegoods. But none of these structures is visible above the surface of the ground, for without consolidation excavated sites must be backfilled in order to prevent collapse. Coastal erosion in the early 1990s revealed a Viking boat-burial at Scar in Sanday, which was excavated only just in time before the force of the sea tore away the rest of the grave.

Late Norse monuments of the 12th century have been included in earlier sections of the book: St Magnus Cathedral, the various smaller churches and hogback tombstones and Cubbie Roo's Castle. As in Scandinavia, it is normally considered that the Viking age in Scotland covers the period from about AD 800 to about AD 1150, although Scandinavian influence on the islands remained strong for several centuries later. Stones inscribed with the Scandinavian runic alphabet have been found in a number of places, including the Brough of Birsay, but these have mostly been gathered into museums; of those still in their original location, the marvellous collection of runes inscribed on the walls of Maes Howe neolithic chambered tomb (no. 72) and the brief inscription on one of the stones of the Ring of Brodgar (no. 64) have been described under the appropriate monuments later in the book.

One of the many runic inscriptions in Maes Howe

Although there are few major Viking-age monuments in terms of surviving visible structure, it is impossible not to be aware, as one explores the islands, of the strength and impact of the Scandinavian colonisation, simply by absorbing place-names and their implications. As you wait for the ferry at Tingwall on the east coast of Orkney mainland (HY 403228), think of all that the name implies; Old Norse *thingvollr* means parliament field, where leading Norsemen gathered to discuss legal business. Was it held here because this place was central between the great families of mainland and those of the islands?

Given the special importance of the sea as a means of transport and communication to the Vikings, it is not surprising that most of their settlements are located close to the coast and close to good landing places for boats. In Orkney, the Bay of Birsay, the Bays of Swandro and Westness on Rousay, Sandside Bay at Skaill in Deerness, the Bays of Pierowall and Tuquoy on Westray are all confirmed by excavations to have been foci of Norse settlement.

It is very noticeable that Viking-age farms were often built literally on top of the ruins of earlier native sites, perhaps as a lazy way of getting building-stone or perhaps out of inbred habit, good land being at such a premium along the fjords of their west Norwegian homelands that it was normal to rebuild on exactly the same spot. The habit was taken to absurd lengths at Saevar Howe in Birsay (HY 245269), where in the 9th century Norsemen built houses perched on top of a huge, tell-like mound that contained the ruins of Pictish and earlier buildings; the ruined Norse buildings were in their turn capped by a cemetery of long cist graves (stone-lined graves) in the 10th century.

Early Viking-Age houses on the Brough of Birsay

The pattern of settlement during the Viking Age was essentially one of scattered farmsteads rather than villages, though the presence of a large cemetery of pagan graves excavated in the 19th century at Pierowall on Westray may suggest that a small hamlet existed there. The typical farm of the 9th and 10th centuries consisted of an oblong dwelling house, known as a hall-house, with separate out-buildings which might include a byre, a stable, a threshing barn and other storehouses, and even a bath-house. If the farm were occupied over several centuries, as at Jarlshof in Shetland, it is possible to trace the inevitable modifications and rebuildings that took place, and to see that, by the end of the 11th century, the true longhouse was becoming fashionable, with the addition to one end of the dwelling-house of a byre. In late Norse times from the 12th century onwards, houses became more complex in design with extra rooms and porches attached to their long walls.

The economic basis of such farms differed little from that of later times, or indeed from that of the existing native population of the islands: cattle, sheep and pigs were reared, and the sea was exploited both for fish and for shellfish to use as fish-bait. Cereal crops were cultivated, including bere (barley) and oats, and sometimes flax was grown so that linen cloth could be made. On the face of it, a normal farming life, essentially self-sufficient apart from some bartered goods such as soapstone, cooking vessels or metal tools and jewellery. But there was another side to Viking life, one which continued even into the 12th century. This was raiding, the true viking expeditions for adventure and plunder. *Orkneyinga Saga* describes how one such farmer-viking lived, Svein Asleifarson: `Winter he would spend at home on Gairsay, where he entertained some eighty men at his own expense. His drinking hall was so big, there was nothing in Orkney to compare with it. In the spring he had more than enough to occupy him with a great deal of seed to sow which he saw to carefully himself. Then when that job was done, he would go off plundering in the Hebrides and in Ireland on what he called his `spring trip', then back home just after midsummer, where he stayed till the cornfields had been reaped and the grain was safely in. After that he would go off raiding again, and never came back till the first month of winter was ended. This he used to call his `autumn-trip'. Such expeditions added all sorts of exotic goods to Norse homes, for merchant ships carrying fine cloth, wine and other imports were as much targets for attack as houses on land.

Nor should the extensive foreign travels of many Norsemen be forgotten as a source of exotic goods and ideas; they went on pilgrimages to Rome and beyond and on crusades to the Holy Land in the 11th and 12th centuries, as the round church at Orphir (no. 39) recalls with its design based on the church of the Holy Sepulchre in Jerusalem, and there was constant traffic between the far-flung Atlantic colonies. A runic inscription in Tankerness House Museum, which is likely originally to have come from the 12th-century church at Orphir, has been shown to contain a very special form of the r-rune, unknown outside Greenland apart from this example and another from Trondheim in Norway - this would seem to imply the presence in Orkney of a Norseman from one of the Greenland settlements.

Pictish Orkney

When the first Viking longships were sighted off the coasts of Orkney and Shetland in the last decade of the 8th century, the islands were Pictish in their material culture and political affiliations, and it seems likely that, as with the later earldom and bishopric, the centre of power lay in Orkney, possibly at Birsay. It is also likely that Orkney had close connections with Caithness in Pictish times as it did in Viking times. Unfortunately, little of the Pictish culture of the islands can be seen on the ground. None of the distinctive Pictish symbol stones remains in its original position, although there is a cast on site of the Brough of Birsay stone (no. 49), and the informal symbol stone, perhaps a trial piece, found at Gurness may be seen in the visitor centre there (no. 53). Given the effect of acid rain and other modern pollution, it is safer for such stone carving to be in museums, and the exceptionally fine stone from the Knowe of Burrian on the east side of the Loch of Harray (HY 308168) is in Tankerness House Museum in Kirkwall.

The exquisitely carved Pictish symbol stone from the Knowe of Burrian

(Far left)
This Pictish symbol stone was found built into St Peter's Church in South Ronaldsay

In the same museum are all the finds and a model of one of the Pictish houses excavated at Buckquoy, beneath the Norse farm already mentioned. Other Pictish buildings have been discovered at Birsay, on the Brough (no. 49), elsewhere on the Point of Buckquoy and on Saevar Howe, and at Howe, near Stromness, Skaill in Deerness and Pool in Sanday, but none is now visible.

At Howe, the Pictish settlement was the final phase in a very long sequence of activity stretching back through a broch to a neolithic chambered tomb and settlement, a most important site.

Several designs for houses seem to have been favoured by the Picts in the Northern Isles: one is shaped in a figure-of-eight as at Buckquoy, another is the cellular type to be seen at Gurness, where small cells are arranged round a central living area, and elsewhere multi-roomed buildings of no particular standard shape seem to have been used, the rooms sometimes rectangular rather than round. Single farmsteads were the normal social unit, and rearing cattle, sheep and pigs, cultivating the land and fishing were the normal life-style. The best-preserved and most typical Pictish house to visit is at Gurness (no. 53), where again it formed a late phase on a major broch site. It is likely that many broch sites where there are extensive remains of outbuildings would on excavation yield evidence of Pictish occupation long after the broch itself had ceased to be used, for instance at Borwick (no. 50) where excavation in the 19th century yielded a typical Pictish comb.

Brochs

Several hundred brochs are known to have existed as a distinctive class of structure that is unique to Scotland, and they were concentrated in northern Scotland and the Western and Northern Isles. They are circular

The figure-of-eight Pictish house at Buckquoy

stone-built structures, with a single door at ground-level and no windows, which seem to have been two storeys or more in height. Some were undoubtedly defensive towers but others may have been simply fortified houses. Their walls are characterised by immense thickness, and by a technique of building the wall, at least above basal level, as two skins with a hollow space between, the skins bonded together at intervals by lintel slabs; this hollow-wall technique allowed greater height to be achieved than would be possible with an entirely solid wall. There are often storage cells built into the thickness of the wall at ground-level, and guard-cells on either side of the entrance passage.

In the case of most excavated brochs, the work was done, often very unscientifically, in the 19th century, and little is known of the sequence of building, but recent excavations in Orkney have clarified several points. The internal design of brochs seems to have been as carefully thought out as the main fabric, with a ground floor laid out round a central hearth, cooking tank and water cistern, and the perimeter subdivided into areas with specific functions by radial slab partitions. Upper floors would be built of timber, probably as galleries rather than complete floors. The earliest dated example is the demolished site at Bu, near Stromness, where the broch was evidently a fortified roundhouse, the home of a single farming family around 600 BC, and it seems that the idea of the broch was then developed further until, by the turn of the millennium, many were indeed fortified towers and some were surrounded by small villages of domestic buildings (as at Gurness, no. 53) and outer defences formed by ramparts and ditches.

Many, but not all, brochs were built in coastal locations, which has led to the idea that they were built against some sea-borne threat. That brochs were defensive in character is indisputable, and, now that their development can be seen as having taken place gradually over some eight to nine centuries (in the Northern Isles at least), they can be appreciated as a facet of the increasing turbulence and internecine warfare that characterises this period throughout the Celtic world.

Forts without brochs were also used, where easily defended promontories have been fortified with one or more lines of rampart and ditch, eg Castle of Burwick (no. 56), but these are rare in Orkney.

A modern sea-wall protects the broch of Midhowe from coastal erosion

Earth-houses

The alternative French term, souterrain, is often used for these subterranean structures which have been found in northern, western and eastern Scotland, Ireland, Cornwall and Brittany. Their design varies regionally, as do their function and date, and even the most common factor, being underground, varies from being totally underground and invisible on the surface to being semi-subterranean with timber-framed roofs at ground-level. It is not, therefore, possible to generalise about them, and they should be seen in their regional context. Earth-houses in the Northern Isles appear to have been small and entirely subterranean (they have often been discovered when the weight of a tractor above has caused their roofs to collapse), to have acted as cool storerooms for domestic settlements and to date to the first millennium BC (although it should be admitted that dating evidence is scanty). Neither of the two Orcadian examples in state care can be precisely dated (nos 57, 58), and the burials found at Rennibister (no. 58) remain a tantalising glimpse of some otherwise undocumented human tragedy.

The stone chapel (before excavation) and oblong houses on the Brough of Deerness can be seen clearly from the air

48 Brough of Deerness, Chapel and Settlement

Viking Age.

HY 596087. From Kirkwall take the A 960 and B 9050 to Skaill, and a minor road N to the carpark. Signposted path.

Orkney Islands Council.

This is one of the most spectacularly located monuments in Orkney, for it occupies the flat top of a large detached rock stack off a coast of precipitous cliffs. Inherent in its location is danger for the unwary visitor, although the character of the site can be appreciated from the adjacent mainland without crossing on to the stack itself. When the various structures were built and in regular use, it is likely that the Brough was accessible along a narrow neck of land, perhaps even at groundlevel, but now that land bridge has eroded away and the path leading up on to the Brough starts virtually on the beach.

A bank runs along the landward side of the Brough, with an entrance towards the south-west corner opposite the adjacent promontory. Such an attempt to control access to the site seems unnecessary today, but, if the Brough was connected to the mainland by a land-bridge, it would have been essential. The major upstanding feature is the chapel within its square enclosure, which was the focus for pilgrimage throughout the Middle Ages and as late as the mid 19th century, although its dedication is unknown. Its visibility from the mainland made it a convenient target for gun practice in the Second World War, resulting in the shell-holes that now pit the area between the bank and the chapel.

To the west and north of the chapel are many grass-grown foundations of rectangular buildings, most of which fall into two rows on either side of a 'street' along the west side of the Brough. These have been the subject of scholarly debate for many years: are they the remains of a monastery or are they simply domestic houses of the Norse or later period? Most prefer the latter interpretation, viewing the site as comparable to the settlement on the Brough of Birsay (no. 49). Only the chapel has been excavated, revealing not only that the existing chapel is probably Norse in date but also that it replaced an earlier version built in timber and stone, thought also to be Norse.

It is thus likely that, whatever its status, this stack site was contemporary with the Norse farm at Skaill (see under no. 47).

49 Brough of Birsay, Church and Settlement

12th centuries AD.

HY 239285. A track leads NW from Birsay village round the bay and along the Point of Buckquoy to a carpark at the tip of the promontory. At low tide it is possible to walk along a causeway to the island; signposted.

Historic Scotland.

To see the Brough of Birsay in summer is to appreciate its attraction for settlement: as a tidal island it is defensible and yet not isolated, and it is situated so as to enjoy all the advantages of this favoured corner of Orkney with its fertile land and sheltered landing places. The island is about 21 hectares in extent, sloping up from about 4 m OD on its east side to the sheer western cliffs, some 45m high, where puffins live. The gentle slope facing mainland belies the incredible force of the

The Brough of Birsay and the Point of Buckquoy at low tide

Atlantic waves that break against its western face, for in winter the sea-spray rises so high that the entire island is washed by salt water; in Viking times, however, the climate was appreciably better than now, with an average mean temperature about 2°C higher, an enormous boon to the arable farmer and a calming influence on the winter storms.

Although the Brough was undoubtedly already a tidal island by late prehistoric times, there has been appalling coastal erosion over the last eight centuries, and much structural evidence of settlement has been lost into the sea, not only adjacent to the central area of buildings east of the church, where house walls and the boat slipway stop abruptly at the cliff edge, but also along the coast on either side. Recent excavations have concentrated on recording what is left of Viking-age and Pictish building along the cliff-edge and on the slice of land that will one day collapse into the sea, known as the Peerie Brough, the little Brough. This means that what has survived as a substantial archaeological site was originally considerably more extensive.

In Norse times, from around AD 800 until the 12th century or perhaps a little later, there was a major settlement here which must always have possessed a rather different status and character from the normal farm, if only because normal farming was impossible on the tiny island itself and must have been supplemented by the produce of fields and pastures on the adjacent mainland. It is possible that the home farm during the 9th century was the site which has been excavated but which is no longer visible on the Point of Buckquoy, where a dwelling-house, barn-byre and threshing barn were discovered. Cattle, sheep and pigs were reared on the Buckquoy farm, whereas the animal bones from excavations on the Brough suggest very logically that sheep were probably grazed on the island itself and beef was brought over ready slaughtered as joints.

The visible buildings are dominated by the church, a fine Romanesque creation which was probably built in the early 12th century; it is very small (the nave is only 8.5 m by 5.8 m internally) but is design is quite sophisticated, with a square chancel and a semi-circular apse at the east end and traces of a probable square tower at the west end. There are semi-circular recesses for altars in the nave, on either side of the chancel arch, and the main altar, which was originally in the apse, is now in the chancel, whence it was moved in later medieval times when the church was a place of pilgrimage (the altar has also been restored in modern times). The proportions of the church and the warm colour of the sandstone are very pleasing, and the stone bench lining the north, south and west walls of the nave gives an excellent impression of its internal lay-out in the days before wooden pews.

Brough of Birsay: 12th-century buildings east of the church

Brough of Birsay: church and 12th-century domestic buildings (Top)

To the north of the church are three ranges of buildings which, with the church on its fourth side, enclose a courtyard. This is thought by some scholars to have formed the kernel of a Benedictine monastery, although unfortunately there is no documentary evidence to identify with certainty either its monastic status or the order to which the monastery belonged. The foundation of this early medieval church represents a return to an ecclesiastical status, for the site had an Early Christian chapel in pre-Norse times, but during the intervening 300 years the settlement is likely to have been purely secular.

At one time the church was thought to be the Christchurch built by Earl Thorfinn after his pilgrimage to Rome around 1050 and the buildings to the north of the church to be the Bishop's Palace of the earliest bishops of the Northern Isles, but it is now agreed that the church was built more than half a century later and that Christchurch and the seat of the bishopric were on the mainland beneath the modern village of Birsay (see no. 38).

The major problem in trying to analyse the various upstanding buildings on the Brough is that the original excavations of the 1930s and 1950s have never been published, apart from a catalogue and discussion of the marvellous range of small finds. The complex of domestic structures to the east of the church represents a sequence spanning the 9th to 12th centuries to judge from the finds. The isolated houses upslope from the church appear to be normal Viking-age domestic hall-houses. Later excavations along the cliff-edge in the 1970s and 1980s have expanded our understanding of this important settlement.

Prior to the arrival of the Norsemen, there was a thriving Pictish community on the island; it is sometimes assumed to have been monastic, because of traces of an earlier chapel beneath the surviving church and earlier graves in the graveyard (literally at a lower level than the later graves), but the chapel may have served a lay community. Few structural traces of the Pictish settlement have been found, perhaps because, unexpectedly, they appear to have been timber-built, apart from the small stone-lined well to the east of the church; although it is only 0.75 m deep, it seems to have provided a water-supply for a bronze-workshop in the vicinity, for the area round about, when excavated in the 1930s, yielded many fragments of broken moulds, crucibles and bronze plating. Prestigious objects were being made here, mostly brooches, finger-rings and dress-pins, and they imply wealthy patronage. Elsewhere in Scotland, such metalworking is associated with the fortified residences of Dark-Age chieftains, such as Dunadd in Argyll, and it seems likely that the Brough, which is in a sense defended by the sea, was also the seat in the 8th century of an important chieftain, perhaps the chieftain depicted on the symbol stone.

The original symbol stone was found shattered into fragments and it is now in the Royal Museum of Scotland in Edinburgh, but a cast has been put up on site. It is an unusual stone in its composition of

design and combination of carving techniques: at least four incised Pictish symbols occupied the upper part of the slab, while incised in a shallow recessed panel beneath are three warriors. The symbols are common enough in the Pictish repertoire: a circular decorated disc which is part of the so-called 'mirror case' symbol, a crescent and V-rod, a 'swimming elephant' or Pictish beast, and an eagle; the bearded warriors are carved with a fine attention to detail, each dressed in a long tunic with sword-belt and a sword-scabbard hanging at their left sides, each carrying a tall spear and a square shield. The rivets holding the hand-grip to the back of the shields are shown as pairs of circles, and the shield held by the leading warrior is decorated. The leader is also distinguished by the decorative hem of his tunic, by the size of his spear (even the midrib of his cast metal spearhead is indicated), and by his curls.

Brough of Birsay: this small building with its slab kerbing may have been a sauna, in which water would have been thrown over hot stones in the centre of the room (Left)

50 Broch of Borwick

Mid 1st millennium AD-late 1st millennium BC.

HY 224167. About 6 km N of Stromness on the B 9056, take the minor road W of Yesnaby. Park at the end of the road, and walk N about 1 km along the cliff-top; the broch is clearly visible from the Hill of Borwick.

The broch-builders chose a place of natural strength, not only on account of the steep cliffs but also because of its proximity to a freshwater burn and a landing-place for boats. The landward side was originally protected by a wall, and 19th-century excavations revealed traces of outbuildings and artefacts showing that the occupation of the site continued into the mid 1st millennium AD. Severe erosion has destroyed the seaward half of the broch, but the eastern half is well preserved and includes the entrance with its door-check half-way long the passage and guard-cell opening off the northern side of the passage. Above the roofing slabs is a small cell. The outer wall-face of the broch is well built, using some massive boulders at the base and smaller slabs above; it survives to a height of almost 3 m.

The Pictish symbol stone from the Brough of Birsay (Left)

The Broch of Borwick on its precipitous headland

51 Broch of Burrian, North Ronaldsay

Mid 1st millennium AD - late 1st millennium BC

HY 762513. On the shore at the S tip of the island; access along the foreshore.

The seaward side of the broch has suffered inevitable erosion, compounded by the fact that it has been incorporated into the island's sheep dyke, the wall that keeps the seaweed-eating sheep on the foreshore. But the broch is still an impressive monument, its wall more than 3 m high, and traces on the landward side of four concentric ramparts. There appear not to have been guard-cells flanking the passage leading into the broch, only a small cell opening from the interior at groundlevel. Oddly the ledge on which the first floor would have been supported is at a height of only 1 m above the floor and about 1.3 m above the ledge the wall is stepped inwards, both features difficult to explain in terms of how the interior of the broch was arranged. There is also an underground well or storage chamber.

Excavations in the early 1870s were of a better standard than was often the case, and they produced a large collection of artefacts, spanning iron-age and Pictish times, as well as bones of cattle, sheep, pig, dog and horse. There was clearly re-use of the site in the 7th and 8th centuries AD, not only within the broch but also in domestic structures outside.

52 Broch of Burroughston, Shapinsay

Early 1st millennium AD - late 1st millennium BC

HY 540210. Signposted from the B 9058 at the NE tip of the island.

Orkney Islands Council.

Plan of the Broch of Burrian

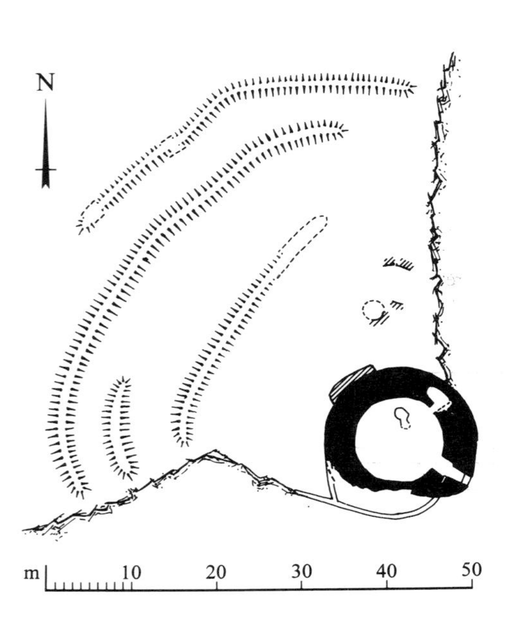

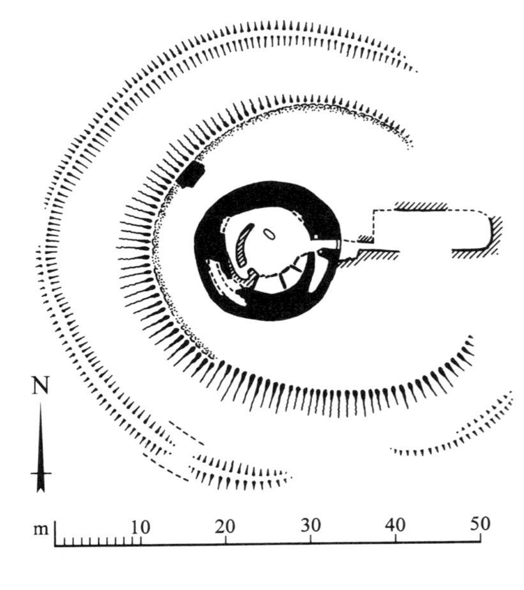

Plan of the Broch of Burroughston (Far right)

Close to the shore with its entrance facing out to sea, this fine broch survives in part to above first-floor level and has been restored (see p.00). The entrance passage has checks and a bar-hole for a door, and a guard-cell on the left on entering. There are the remains of radial compartments inside the broch, along with a 3 m-deep well, and projecting from the wall is the ledge which helped to support the first floor. The interior was cleared out in the 1860s with little record.

Surrounding the broch is a strong defence of concentric wall, ditch and rampart, which, from an old plan, appears originally to have encircled the site entirely, perhaps making up for the lack of natural defence on this low coast. The ground outside the broch is very uneven, and there have clearly been other buildings in the space between the broch and its defences.

53* Broch of Gurness

9th century AD-1st century BC.

HY 381268. From the A 966 between Finstown and Birsay, take the minor road NE to the carpark; signposted.

Historic Scotland.

Gurness has the most extensive and well-preserved domestic buildings surrounding the broch to be seen anywhere in Scotland, and these, together with the visitor centre and a superb view across Eynhallow Sound to Rousay, make this monument a truly fascinating place to visit (it is also a very exposed location needing a reasonably calm day to enjoy it). The first buildings that one encounters after entry to the site, close to the visitor centre, are in fact the latest in the sequence. Before excavation the entire site was a huge grassy mound, and these buildings were found at a high level in the mound, to the north-east of the underlying broch. They were dismantled and re-built in their present position. One is an excellent example of a Pictish house in which five cells surround a central livingroom, and the other is a large oblong house, which has often been assumed to be a Norse hall-house but which could equally well be Pictish (artefacts associated with it are unfortunately undiagnostic). There was certainly activity on the site in the Viking age, because a female grave with typical Scandinavian brooches was discovered inserted into the old rampart surrounding the broch (her gravegoods may be seen in Tankerness House Museum: a pair of oval bronze brooches, an iron necklet, an iron sickle and an iron knife with a wooden handle).

Coastal erosion has destroyed the northernmost part of the site, but it is likely that the outer defences of the broch, a wide band of three ramparts and three ditches, originally encircled the broch completely, with an entrance causeway still surviving on the east side. The broch itself was almost certainly built as a tall tower, but its walls have been much reduced in height, probably as a source of building stone; it has a solid wall-base, with cells within the wall on either side of the

The broch and its village were enclosed within a stone wall and outer ramparts and ditches

The Broch of Gurness from the air, with the Pictish cellular house to the right (Top)

Part of the Gurness village

An entrance way leads through the village to the broch (Top)

entrance. The layout on the ground-floor has been complicated by later modifications, but the original design included a well-constructed rectangular hearth and steps leading down to a subterranean cellar with a water-tank fed by a spring, both of which still survive.

Surrounding the broch and filling the entire space available within the outer defences is a remarkable series of semi-detached houses, which, it has been estimated, might have been the homes of some 30-40 families. The construction of these buildings takes every advantage of the available stone, using large upright slabs as well as horizontal drystone masonry. Although secondary in the overall sequence of building, it is thought that these houses were inhabited contemporary with the use of the broch, and their arrangement neatly respects the pathway leading from the broch out through the ramparts and ditches.

54 Broch of Lamb Ness, Stronsay

HY 690214. From the end of the B 9060 at the SE end of the island, take the minor road to Cleat and walk S for about 1 km to Lamb Ness.

Although this is not one of Orkney's best-preserved brochs, it is worth a visit for its location and for other features of interest in the vicinity. The broch stands above dramatic sea-cliffs appropriately named Hells Mouth on the south side of Lamb Bay. It was partially excavated in the 19th century, but nothing is known of the interior, except that there appear to be structures of later date within it, or of any finds. The entrance on the north-west is visible, as are the well-built guard-cells on either side, which still survive some 2 m high.

Close to the shore on the west side of the promontory is a ruined chambered cairn (HY 689212), in which the tops of slabs forming part of a stalled chamber can be seen in an oval cairn about 12 m long. Another mound just to the west is probably the remains of some domestic structure. Farther north, towards the narrow neck of the promontory, there are good examples of kelp-pits and kelp-drying stances, and a curious L-shaped bank of boulders projects from the shore into the Bay of Houseby. Known as the Danes' Pier, tradition would have this to be an artificial jetty, but it is more likely to be natural.

55 Midhowe Broch, Rousay

c 2nd century AD-c 2nd century BC.

HY 371306. From Brinyan pier, take the B 9064 NW for about 8 km, then follow footpath downhill; signposted.

Historic Scotland.

Midhowe is an excellent example of a broch built on a promontory with outer defences on the landward side, here consisting of a truly massive stone-built rampart with a ditch on either side. The area thus enclosed was originally larger than it survives now, for there has been considerable erosion and loss of external buildings on the west side of the broch. The sea wall built to protect the

The Broch of Midhowe from the air - building slabs had only to be prised up from the bedrock of the foreshore

ite in the 1930s is itself a superb building .chievement, utilising to the full the qualities of the ocal flagstone. Nevertheless, the design of the roch and its defences is so compact, with the wall f the broch only a couple of metres from the inner litch, that there can be no doubt that this was built .s a prestigious, fortfied family house - the iron-age quivalent of the Norse castle on Wyre (no. 36). The external buildings round the broch were added ater, when defence was no longer as vital, for they re built over the filled-in ditch and directly against he rampart itself.

nstead of having a solid wall-base, the broch has a allery within the wall at ground-level, a design hat seems not to have been entirely successful ecause at some stage the gallery had partially to e filled with rubble and external buttressing to be uilt against the outer wall-face on the north side n order to prevent serious collapse (the buttressing vas achieved by stacking vertical slabs just as in the 0th-century sea-wall, the same solution to similar roblems almost 2000 years apart). The broch wall urvives to a height of 4.3 m, with an internal ledge or a first-floor gallery at a height of just over 3 m, nd the layout of the ground-floor is particularly nteresting and well-preserved, bearing in mind hat its present appearance reflects the final phase of its occupation and may not be entirely representative of earlier phases. Tall slabs were used to divide the somewhat crowded interior into two semi-circular rooms, each then subdivided further into cells and cupboards, and each with its hearth and stone-built water-tank. The main hearth in the southern room even retains the stone-lined post-hole on either side which held the uprights for a spit over the fire, from which pots might be hung or joints of meat roasted. The underground cellar in the northern room may have been used for storing food supplies or it may once have been fed by a spring to be a freshwater supply. Perhaps the most remarkable feature of the broch interior is the alcove built to the immediate north of the entrance, a superb demonstration of some ancient stone-mason's skill and mastery of his resources. Balanced on a tall thin flagstone, itself almost 2.3 m high, is a pier of drystone masonry which soars upwards to become a corbelled ceiling to the alcove.

Sufficient remains of the first floor of the broch to give a graphic impression of its arrangements. The stone ledge projecting from the broch-wall round the eastern half of the broch helped to support a wooden gallery (further support being provided by timber posts), to which there must have been access

Buttressing was added outside the broch to prevent collapse

by means of a wooden ladder in the northern room, which also gave entry via a doorway in the broch-wall to a stairway and upper gallery within the thickness of the wall. At a later stage, a stone stair was built in the southern room leading to a cell in the wall at first-floor level, which also had the effect of blocking the upper gallery in the wall. The timber-built first-floor was presumably used as sleeping accommodation, the ground-floor being taken up with cooking and storage facilities, while the stairs and gallery within the broch wall provided a means of access to the top of the broch-tower.

Among the stones chosen by the broch-builders are two cup-marked boulders which were probably carved sometime in the second or early first millennium BC. One is built into the south face of a fragmentary structure to the south of the broch, and the other, which is decorated with both cups and rings, is built into the outer face of the broch itself, low down on its north-north-east side. These two stones may well have been associated originally with the nearby chambered tomb (no. 81).

In common with most excavated brochs in Orkney, many artefacts were found in and around the broch, including some of Roman origin: sherds of distinctive pottery and fragments of a typical bronze ladle. The Northern Isles were well beyond the limits of Roman control in Scotland, and the presence of Roman objects such as these must be seen in the context of gifts, trade or raiding, probably not directly with the Romans but through intermediate native contacts. Other finds included a variety of bone and stone tools and bronze jewellery (now in NMS), and there was evidence to show that both bronze and iron had been manufactured on the site, including an iron-smelting hearth in one of the external buildings. Without the help of radiocarbon analysis, dating of this particular broch is likely to err on the conservative side, for several aspects of its design and later development suggest that it may well have been one of the earliest Orcadian brochs to be built as a true tower.

One of the domestic buildings outside the broch

The Ladykirk Stone (Far left)

56 Castle of Burwick, Fort, South Ronaldsay

? Late 1st millennium BC.

ND 434842. Follow the A 961 from Kirkwall to very end at Burwick, and walk W for 0.5 km to the coast.

The Castle of Burwick is almost an island, for it is joined to the mainland only by a very narrow neck of land, although this may have been somewhat wider in iron-age times, and the cliffs are high and sheer. Three lines of rampart with ditches between them have been built on mainland to guard access to the fort, and a fourth rampart lies across the approach on the fort side; in the long grass within the forts, there are traces of structures, presumably houses, beneath the turf.

Preserved within St Mary's Church at Burwick is an oval boulder, known as the Ladykirk Stone, which is carved with a pair of footprints, but its original provenance is unfortunately unknown. Elsewhere in Scotland such carved foot-prints (always of shod feet) are thought to be associated with ceremonies surrounding the inauguration of Dark-Age kings, symbolising the idea that the new king will follow in the footsteps of the old. Although the power-centre of Pictish Orkney is thought to be the Brough of Birsay (no. 49), there may have been more than one such centre, and it is not impossible that Castle of Burwick was in use at this time.

The entrance passage into Grain earth-house was partially rock-cut

57* Grain, Earth-house, Kirkwall

1st millennium BC.

HY 441116. In an industrial estate on the NW outskirts of Kirkwall, approached by a minor road leading E off the A 965 just beyond the causeway between the harbour and the Peerie Sea; signposted.

Historic Scotland.

This earth-house has remained in excellent condition, probably because it was constructed so deeply underground. Some 2 m of earth separates its roof from the ground-surface, and a flight of steps leads down into the passage (the upper part

Inside the chamber at Grain

of the stair is modern but the lower part is original). The passage curves in a gentle arc, lined with drystone walling and roofed by flat lintels at a height of about 0.9 m, so that it is impossible to walk upright, but it opens into a well-built oval chamber which is just high enough, at 1.6 m, for most people to move about upright or almost upright. As a cellar for storing food supplies, comfort was not an important factor. The flat lintelled roof is supported on four free-standing pillars of stone.

When it was discovered in the 19th century, the earth-house was empty, but clear evidence was found of there having been a domestic settlement at ground-level: the basal courses of walls and a large pit full of ash, burnt wood, animal bones and shells. In 1982 a second smaller earth-house was discovered about 6 m to the west, which presumably belonged to the same settlement, but this is no longer visible.

58 Rennibister, Earth-house

1st millennium BC.

HY 397125. Some 6.5 km WNW of Kirkwall on the A 965, signposted with carpark; the earth-house is in the yard of a working farm, and cars should not be taken into the farmyard.

Historic Scotland.

An interesting example of a modern farm on exactly the same spot as an iron-age farm. Rennibister lies close to the shore with access to a fertile area of land which has attracted settlement since neolithic times as demonstrated by three chambered cairns. Another earth-house was found in the 19th century near Saverock, between Rennibister and Grain. The presence of the earth-house at Rennibister was unsuspected until 1926 when its roof gave way beneath the weight of a threshing-machine passing overhead, and a modern hatch and ladder now allow entry through the roof into the chamber. Original access was down the narrow lintelled passage opening into the opposite end of the chamber, though with a width and height of only about 0.7 m, it can never have been easy. The chamber is oval, its originally corbelled roof supported on four free-standing stone pillars and its walls are furnished with five small recesses, one divided by a stone shelf. When it was first discovered, the end of the passage was filled with shells and domestic refuse, and a jumbled mass of human bones on the floor of the chamber proved to be the remains of six adults and twelve children. The fact that the skeletons were disarticulated implies that it was as bones rather than bodies that they were placed in the earth-house, presumably having originally been buried elsewhere, but it is not known why, or when, this was done.

Rennibister earth-house: chamber and entrance passage

Plan and section of Rennibister (Far right)

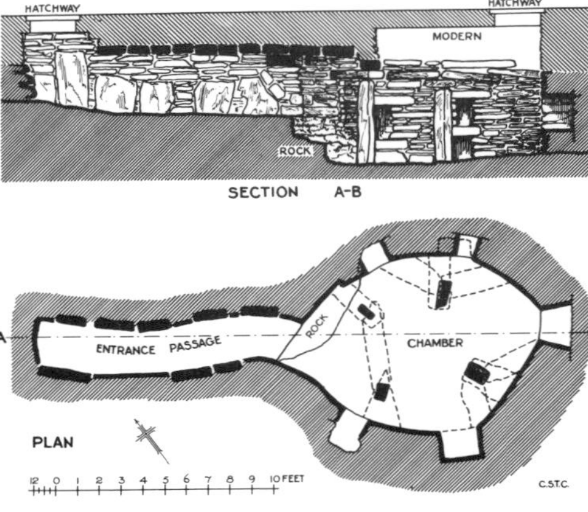

8 LIFE IN EARLY PREHISTORIC TIMES

Skaill Bay and the neolithic village of Skara Brae

One of the great joys of visiting the Northern Isles must be the insight into early prehistoric times offered by a variety of outstandingly well-preserved monuments that have somehow survived fifty or more centuries of human impact on their environment. Where else in north-west Europe can you hope to find the houses of people who lived and toiled 5000 years ago still standing to eaves level? Neolithic houses are rarely encountered above ground-level in the rest of the British Isles, and excavation yields few details of their interiors to match the stone-built furniture of Skara Brae. The great standing stones, long part of the folklore of the islands, became widely known through the drawings and writing of early travellers from the 18th century onwards. Sir Walter Scott staged the final scenes of his novel *The Pirate* at the Stones of Stenness, and the discovery of Skara Brae has inspired many a poet and storyteller of the 20th century.

Burnt Mounds

Judged by quantity alone, burnt mounds would be the single most important class of prehistoric monument in Orkney, for more than 200 are known to exist or to have existed in the past, and yet little attention was paid to them until the 1970s when two were fully excavated. Before excavation, burnt mounds appear literally as mounds of burnt and shattered stone and black soil, grass-grown but often with burnt stones visible here and there, and they are always located near a source of freshwater; in size they vary from a few metres to 30 m or more across, and

The great stone circle at Brodgar

they are often crescentic in shape. Classic examples are mentioned in the Papa Westray excursion at Backiskaill and in the Stromness to Birsay excursion at Fan Knowe near Dounby, and an excavated example may be seen in South Ronaldsay at Liddle (no. 59).

Burnt mounds are in fact cooking places, where stones were heated on a hearth and thrown into troughs of water so as to boil the water for cooking large joints of meat; the stones, burnt and cracked, were then discarded in an arc round the cooking area. Cooking was carried out in oval stone-built shelters, which may have been communal cook-houses serving people living close by, and scientific dating of burnt stone and pottery has shown that they were used between about 1000 and 400 BC. Finds of agricultural tools and cereal pollen, together with their distribution on good fertile soil, combine to demonstrate that burnt mounds belonged to farming communities. Very similar mounds occur elsewhere in mainland Scotland, England, Wales and southern Ireland.

Although roasting would seem the simplest method of cooking meat, there is no doubt that boiling was a popular alternative and, amongst people whose pottery was not strong enough to use over the fire and who lacked metal containers, boiling in a stone or wooden trough was acceptably efficient. It had an important advantage over roasting in that the melting fat was not lost into the fire. There is evidence of this type of cooking in early Irish literature and, closer to home, in a description of the Hebrides in the mid 18th century: 'the meaner sort of people still retain the custom of boiling their beef in the hide; or otherwise (being destitute of vessels of metal or earth) they put water into a block of wood made hollow by the help of the dirk and burning; and then with pretty large stones heated red-hot and successively quenched in that vessel, they keep the water boiling, till they have dressed their food.'

A substantial neolithic house at Knap of Howar

Settlements

The archaeological record leaves a distinct impression of material poverty among communities in the Northern Isles during the later 2nd and early 1st millennia BC, and, aside from the prolific burnt mounds, relatively few traces of domestic settlements have been found. A combination of climatic deterioration, bringing with it an increase in the formation of peat and barren moorland, and the effect of intense cultivation in late neolithic times seem to have led to short-term settlement and somewhat insubstantial buildings easily obliterated by later ploughing. In some marginal areas traces survive of field-systems, clearance cairns (piles of stones cleared from the fields) and hut-circles of probable bronze-age date, but it often takes a trained eye to distinguish them on the ground.

In contrast, the substantial settlements and tombs of the earlier 2nd millennium, 3rd and early 4th millennium reflect an era of economic stability amid long-lasting farms, when a milder climate even allowed the cultivation of wheat, and there was the labour and the incentive to build on a grand scale. Skara Brae (no. 61) and Knap of Howar (no. 63) are remarkable both for their preservation and for the wealth of information afforded by their excavation, while Barnhouse has intriguing evidence of social and ritual complexities (no. 62). Traces of plough-furrows have been found at Links of Noltland in Westray, an important settlement hidden beneath the sand-dunes.

Liddle burnt mound during excavation

The stone-lined tank at Liddle (Top right)

Plan of burnt mound at Liddle (Right)

59 Liddle, Burnt Mound, South Ronaldsay

Early 1st millennium BC.

ND 464841. Just before the A 961 terminates at Burwick,the B 9041 leads E; after 1.5 km, take the minor road S to Liddle farm, signposted; c 400 m NE of farmhouse.

This was formerly a very large burnt mound, about 2 m high, which had accumulated round an oval building on a slope above a small burn. The basal courses of the shelter survive to a height of almost a metre, the floor is paved and round the walls is a series of compartments formed by upright slabs, but the major feature is the sunken trough, massively built with thick stone slabs forming the sides and bottom of a watertight box, 1.6 m by 1.0 m and 0.6 m deep. When this trough was first excavated, it was half-full of burnt stones left from the last cooking. The eastern part of the shelter had been disturbed by recent quarrying for road-metal, but sufficient remained of the hearth to show that it had been set in an alcove in the wall and that the fuel used was peat. The position of the hearth suggests that the building was not roofed, for even if the alcove were itself roofed by lintels or corbelling, the danger of setting the rafters alight would be considerable; given the steam that must have been produced by the trough, an enclosed building would have been unbearable to work in, steam and smoke combining to make it impossible either to see or to breathe.

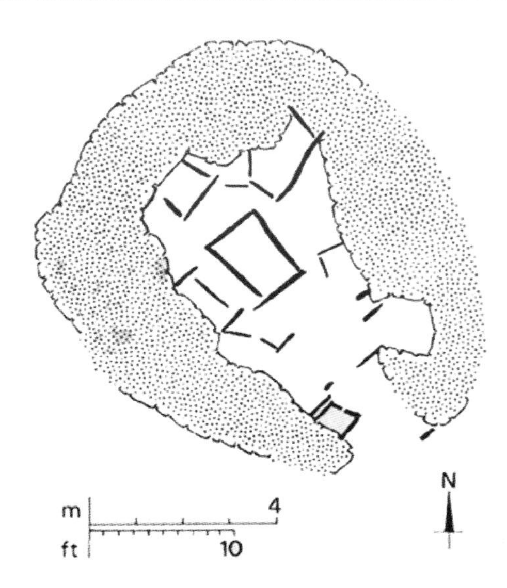

60 Tofts Ness, Settlement, Sanday

3rd and 1st millennia BC.

HY 7647. At the NE end of the island; from the B 9069, a minor road leads N.

The ancient landscape on the promontory of Toft Ness is typical of the extensive remains that ca[n] survive in marginal areas. Before excavation, ther[e] was little indication of the date of this grea[t] complex of large mounds up to 30 m or more i[n] diameter, low enclosure banks and small cairns i[n] their hundreds, apart from some recent kelp kiln and kelp-drying stances. But selective excavatio[n] has identified circular houses and fields of tw[o] main periods, one neolithic and early bronze age and the other spanning the late bronze age and early iron age. From the earliest settlement on the promontory onwards, people were growing cereal crops (even using manure as fertiliser) and breeding cattle and sheep, and by the bronze age they were importing steatite from Shetland.

61* Skara Brae, Settlement

c 2500 BC - c 3100 BC.

HY 231187. Well signposted from several directions, the car park for Skara Brae is near the Bay of Skaill, off the B 9056, on the W coast of mainland.

Historic Scotland.

The west coast of Orkney is mostly very rugged, with high cliffs and pounding Atlantic waves prohibiting coastal settlement, and the only shelter to be found is in the three bays of Birsay, Marwick and Skaill. But the size and shape of these bays has been altered by erosion over the centuries, and the settlement of Skara Brae, when it was founded some 5000 years ago, was certainly not on the shore as it is now but set well back from the sea. Environmental evidence even suggests that a freshwater loch, like the Loch of Skaill behind Skaill House, may have separated the site from the sea and its immediate sandy shore. The name Skara Brae was originally coined to describe the huge sand-dune that covered the site until storm damage in 1850 revealed the presence of stone structures and midden deposits, and, although erosion has destroyed the northern margin of the settlement, it seems likely that the impression given by the visible surviving remains is essentially accurate: this was, architecturally and socially, a tightly knit housing complex for a small community of perhaps fifty people.

Radiocarbon dating suggests that Skara Brae was inhabited for around 600 years, during which time there was rebuilding and modification of the houses and interconnecting passages, and inevitably most of the structures visible today represent the final layout of the village. Its focus consists of six square or rectangular houses linked by narrow irregular passages, very much an inward-looking complex, with a single isolated building of somewhat different design on the west side of the village. The evidence of burnt stones and chips of chert found in this building (no. 8) suggests that it was not an ordinary house but a workshop, probably where chert tools were manufactured

The main passage through the village at Skara Brae

Part of the main passage with its roof intact

A Skara Brae house fully furnished in stone (House 1)

(chert was used as a substitute for flint, which in Orkney occurs only as relatively small nodules washed up on the shore). The main group of domestic houses has two remarkable characteristics: embedded in midden, it is virtually subterranean, and the internal design of its housing units has a standard uniformity. Both aspects were deliberate and, assuming that there was no prehistoric equivalent of a modern building contractor at work here, they must indicate a very strong sense of corporate identity amongst the families of this community.

Behind the dresser on the right was a storage cell (House 5)

Each house consists of a single room with thick drystone walls surviving in some places as high as 3 m. There is a marked contrast between the cramped conditions of the passageways and the equally low and narrow doorways and the spacious and comfortable house-interiors, again a contrast that must have been deliberate and which mirrors the design of contemporary tombs with their low tunnel-like passages and soaring chambers. It is as if the idealogy of their builders demanded that getting there should be humiliatingly difficult but living there, whether in life or death, should be glorious. Small cells were built into the walls, mostly for storage but some furnished with drains as lavatories. A large square hearth with stone kerbs occupies the centre of each house, and the use of stone slabs to build furniture has left us with an unusually precise picture of how the rest of the room was arranged (best seen in nos 1 and 7): slab-built beds flanked either side of the hearth, and a stone dresser was built against the wall opposite the door. Wall cupboards and stone boxes sunk into the floor provide extra storage space. To these bare essentials the visitor's eye should add heather and furs to the beds, skin canopies spanning the bed-posts, decorative pottery jars to the dresser, flame to the hearth, dried meats and fish hanging from the rafters....

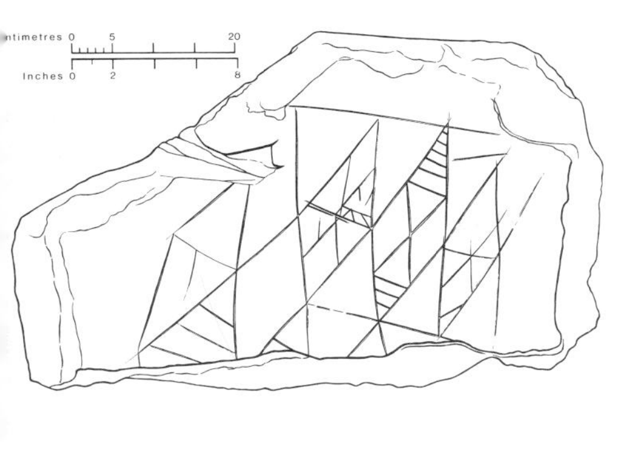

aces of earlier houses suggest a greater variety of an and perhaps less sophisticated interior design: . 9 is the most complete, and it has a central arth and bed-alcoves built into the thickness of e walls. Without demolishing the later houses, it impossible to reconstruct the appearance of the iginal village, but the basic economy and aterial culture of the community seems to have anged little over the centuries, suggesting that the erall form of the settlement probably also mained the same. A self-sufficient life-style was sed on animal husbandry, fishing and cereal ltivation, with thriving local manufacture of one and bone tools and of thick pottery jars own as Grooved Ware, often decorated in relief th spirals, boses and linear motifs. There is a all site museum (where an excellent official idebook is sold) and other finds from the cavations are in Stromness Museum and nkerness House Museum, although the bulk of material is in NMS.

Barnhouse, Settlement

800 BC-3200 BC.

307127. From the A 965 Kirkwall to Stromness d, take the B 9055 N to the carpark for the Stones Stenness (no. 65); a signposted footpath leads to S shore of the Loch of Harray.

kney Islands Council.

ly the lowest courses of these remarkable houses ve survived, partly the result of centuries of ughing and partly because they appear to have en deliberately demolished at the end of their ful life, but the excavated remains have been rebuilt and visitors are able to walk through them (see p.00). Despite the fact that only the base of each house can be seen, the similarity to the better preserved houses at Skara Brae is striking. There are the same central kerbed hearths, bed alcoves and dressers, and drains run from the settlement into the loch. Two of the houses are far more elaborate than those at Skara Brae, perhaps implying a social or ritual hierarchy. Barnhouse and the Stones of Stenness were in use at the same time, and the stone circle and henge may well have been built and serviced by the people living beside the loch. Only part of the settlement has been excavated, and it was clearly both substantial and long-lived.

Decorated stone from Skara Brae
(Left)

63 Knap of Howar, Settlement, Papa Westray

c 2800 BC-3700 BC.

HY 483518. The island can be reached by air or sea from Kirkwall: the airfield is within easy walking distance of the site, and transport to Holland from the pier at the S end can be arranged on arrival. A signposted track leads from Holland to the field in which the site lies.

Historic Scotland.

Approaching across the field, this well-preserved neolithic farmstead is invisible until the visitor is almost upon it, for it lies in a sand-filled pocket of the landscape and, until first excavated in the early 1930s, it was hidden within a 4 m thick blanket of

Knap of Howar neolithic farmstead

Knap of Howar: this house is divided into three rooms, with a slab-built hearth and wall-cupboards

windblown sand. The local topography is very different now from five and a half thousand years ago: environmental evidence, especially the shells of tiny landsnails, indicates that the farmstead lay not on the shore but in open grassland behind a protective system of sand-dunes. Even now the coast of neighbouring Westray is less than 2 km away across a sound that is in places no more than 7 m deep, and it is possible that in neolithic times the two islands were still joined together. Certainly proximity to a bay is implied by the presence in the midden of vast numbers of oyster shells, which thrive only in a sheltered habitat.

This was a small, single-family farmstead relying for a living on breeding cattle and sheep, fishing and growing wheat and barley. The two oblong buildings represent a dwelling-house and a multi-purpose workshop-cum-barn, built side by side with an interconnecting passage allowing access from one to another; they were not the first structures on the site, for they were built into an existing midden, but any earlier buildings were either dismantled or have yet to be discovered. This midden material, compacted into a dense clayey consistency, provided an economic building material, for the thick house-walls have a core of midden, faced on either side with stone.

The dwelling-house is the larger and best-preserved of the two buildings, with its entrance intact and its walls up to 1.6 m high; the doorway at the inn end of the lintelled entrance-passage is furnishe with a sill, jambs and checks to take a wooden doc which would be barred into position. Inside, th house is spacious, 10 m by 5 m, and divided b upright stone slabs (and, originally, timber post into two rooms, the outer having a low stone benc along one wall and the inner acting as the kitche excavation revealed traces of a central heart footings for wooden benches and post-holes fc roof-supports. The great stone quern is still whe it was found, along with another smaller quern: rubbing-stone held in the hand would grind th grain in the hollowed trough. The worksho alongside has a similar though less well-preserve main entrance and, unexpectedly, the door closir the interlinking passage between the two buildin was set in the workshop rather than in the hous Here slabs divide the interior into three rooms, th innermost furnished with shelves and cupboar and the middle room acting as the main worki area, round a central stone-built hearth.

Many domestic artefacts were recovered: bone ar stone tools, sherds of decorative bowls and ja (known as Unstan Ware), all made on the site fro local materials (NMS).

CEREMONIAL CIRCLES AND STANDING STONES

The two henges and stone circles of the Ring Brodgar (no. 64) and the Stones of Stenness (no. 6 should be viewed together, along with the attendant standing stones and barrows, as a gre ceremonial complex in the heart of Orkne comparable to Callanish on Lewis in the Weste Isles and to Stonehenge on Salisbury Plains Wiltshire. Henges are purely British phenomeno occurring as far apart as Cornwall and Orkney a dating to the 3rd millennium BC; they consist of circular or oval bank with a ditch outside i circumference and one or two entrance causeway Sometimes they contain circles of standing stone as at Brodgar and Stenness, and sometimes, more southerly areas where timber is a mo appropriate building material, excavation h revealed the post-holes of timber circles. Th labour and organisation involved in th construction of these two monuments w

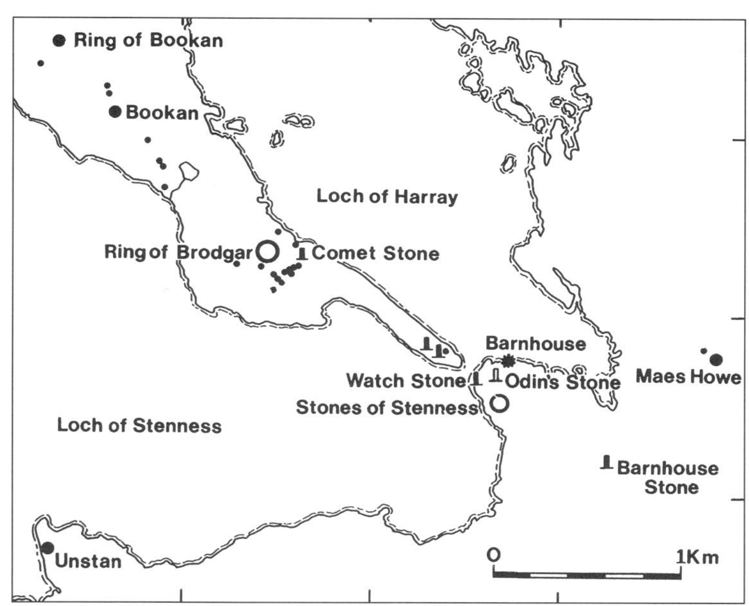

Map of the Brodgar-Stenness ceremonial complex

The rock-cut ditch at the Ring of Brodgar (Top left)

mense: it has been estimated that cutting the odgar ditch involved shifting some 4,700 cubic etres of rock and would have taken about 80,000 an-hours to complete. The concept and nstruction of such public works imply an ganised society united in its cosmology and rhaps united in its allegiance to a high king; it s been argued that, in Orkney, society evolved m small autonomous groups in early neolithic nes to a centralized, hierarchical tribal system ound 3000 BC. The sanctity of the Brodgar-enness area remained potent throughout the 3rd d 2nd millennia, as the various burial mounds d standing stones testify; a cemetery of small ne cists discovered in 1925 yielded an elegantly corated slab, incised with chevrons and lozenges.

anding stones, sometimes in pairs but normally gle, occur frequently in Orkney , but none has en scientifically investigated and little is known their purpose or precise date. They are usually up in conspicuous positions, although not necessarily on the crest of hills or ridges, and the tallest can be 3 m to 5.6 m high above the surface of the ground, implying that their total length, including the portion underground, may well be over 6 m in many cases. Sometimes the tops of the chocking stones are visible, jammed into the pit into which the monolith was set to keep it upright. From evidence elsewhere in Scotland, such stones may be associated with burials and there is some support for this idea in the pair of stones at Brodgar (see under no. 64) which appears to be associated with a burial mound. It is also possible that they were set up as markers of one sort or another, territorial or astronomical, and, on balance, a date in the second millennium BC is most likely, but standing stones are particularly tantalising fragments of an ancient landscape that we cannot hope ever to understand entirely. Several stones have become part of local folklore and have even been used in old customs until within the last century, particularly in the plighting of troths between lovers.

The decorated slab from Ness of Brodgar

Ring of Brodgar from the air

Ring of Brodgar (Top right)

64 Ring of Brodgar, Henge and Stone Circle

3rd millennium BC.

HY 294133. On the A 965, Stromness to Kirkwall road, take the B 9055 NW between the lochs of Stenness and Harray; the Ring is clearly visible in the left and is signposted.

Historic Scotland.

The Ness of Brodgar was a perfect place to choose for a great ceremonial monument, giving the impression of being surrounded by water and sky and yet firmly in the fertile heart of Orkney. Its open location is echoed by the vastness of the circle. In essence, this is a henge monument with two entrances enclosing a prefect circle of standing stones, 103.7 m in diameter; there is no trace of a bank, despite the great volume of rock and soil that must have been dug out of the ditch, about 10 m wide at ground-level and more than 3 m deep (now half-full of silt). In the mid 19th century only fourteen stones were standing, but others have been re-erected so that there are twenty-seven standing, and the positions are known of another thirteen; assuming that the stones were put up at approximately equal distances, it is likely that there were originally sixty stones in the circle. Apart from those surviving as broken stumps, the existing stones vary between about 2 m and 4.5 m in height. It has been suggested that the circle was designed as a lunar observatory, using the Hellia Cliff on Hoy which is outlined on the horizon as a foresight, b the date at which this could have been possible calculated at c 1500 BC, which is almost certain much later than the date of construction. As y there is no precise dating evidence but the early t mid 3rd millennium would be the most like context. There has been no excavation within th circle to discover whether any trace exists internal structures.

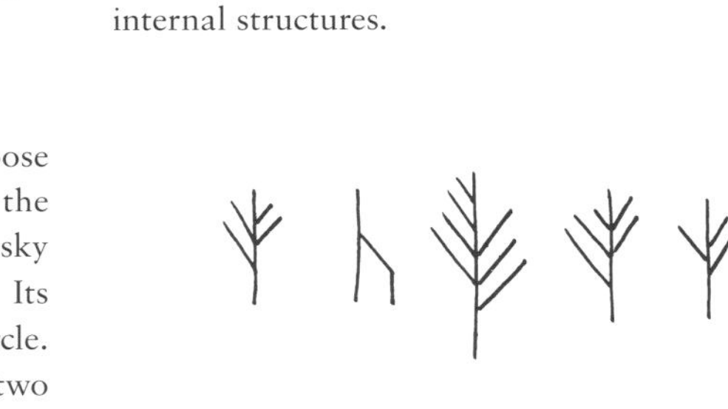

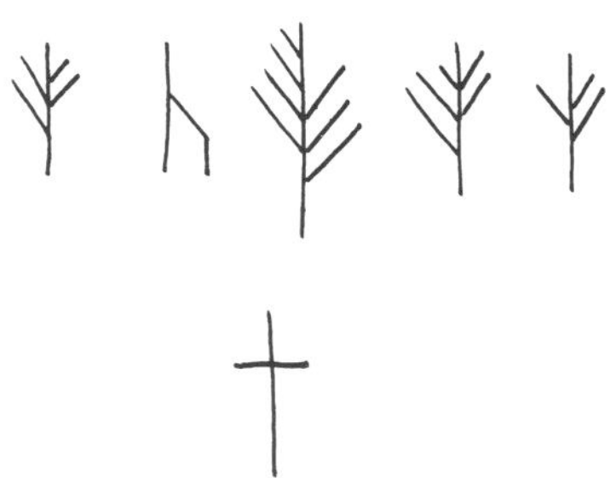

Ring of Brodgar runes (Right)

Sometime in the 12th century, a Norse visit carved his name on the south face of one of th stones in the northernmost arc of the circle (th third stone to the north of the entrance); the sto is now a broken stump, but his runic letters a clear, together with a small cross incised beneat them. These are twig runes or tree runes, so calle from their appearance, and they are cryptograph but easily read by counting the branches on eith side of each rune and then reading off the numb n the following table: counting (from the right) ives 12 (mistakenly written 21 on the rune) 23 34 r s an ordinary rune) 22. Reading from the left-and side and then the top of the table, these pairs f numbers give *biorn*, a common man's name even oday, Bjorn.

	1	2	3	4	5	6
3	f	u	th	o	r	k
2	h	n	i	a	s	
1	t	b	m	l	y	

here are two very large burial mounds to the orth-east of the Ring of Brodgar, between the odern road and the loch, and another large ound, known as Salt Knowe, to the west; smaller ounds are scattered over the Ness of Brodgar om south of the great circle to the Ring of Bookan the north, but very little is known of their ontents or date. Close to the shore of the loch to e north-west of the Ring is a large disc barrow, o-called because the burial mound is surrounded t a short distance by a bank. This type of barrow vas fashionable in southern England but is rarely ound in Scotland, underlining the direct links with e far south that are demonstrated by the rich urial at Knowes of Trotty (no. 69).

North of Brodgar, the Ring of Bookan may be another, smaller henge monument (HY 283144), while to the immediate east is a standing stone known as the Comet Stone, set on a low platform on which the stumps of two more stones are visible. A pair of standing stones, some 8 m apart, adorn the very tip of the promontory near Brodgar farm (HY 303128). It seems likely that in prehistoric times the promontories of Brodgar and Stenness were still joined as a narrow neck of land.

65 The Stones of Stenness, Henge and Stone Circle

Early 3rd millennium BC.

HY 306125. On the A 965, Stromness to Kirkwall road, take the B 9055 NW for just over 0.5 km; the site is close to the E side of the road; signposted.

Historic Scotland.

After suffering deliberate destruction of two of its stones and one of its outlying standing stones (the Stone of Odin) in the early 19th century, restoration was carried out in the early 20th century and four stones of the circle now survive, the tallest over 5 m high. Excavation revealed the bedding-holes for

Stones of Stenness with the Watch Stone in the background

Stones of Stenness: the stone setting at the centre of the circle

The ditch during excavation

other stones, and it is likely that there were originally twelve stones set in a circle about 30 m in diameter. Although ploughing has all but levelled the henge earthworks, the circle once stood within a ditch and bank with an overall diameter of about 44 m and an entrance causeway on the north, and excavation has shown the ditch to be 7 m wide at ground-level and over 2 m deep, cut into to solid rock. In the centre of the circle was found a square setting of flat slabs and, aligned between this and the entrance, the bedding slots for a series of stone and timber uprights, but none of these last features is now visible.

Bones of cattle, sheep and dog were found in the bottom of the ditch, along with one human finger bone, and radiocarbon analysis of the bone indicates that the henge was built in the early 3rd millennium BC, a date confirmed by discovery of Grooved Ware pottery similar to that from the contemporary villages of nearby Barnhouse (no. 62) and Skara Brae, some 10 km to the north-west (no.61).

Two outlying standing stones are likely to have some connection with the henge: the Watch Stone, a magnificent slab, 5.6 m tall, which stands close to the causeway between the two promontories, and the Barnhouse Stone, some 700 m south-east of the circle.

66 Stane o'Quoybune, Standing Stone

2nd millennium BC.

HY 253263. On the A 967 between Twatt and Birsay at the NW extreme of the Loch of Boardhouse, in a field immediately SW of the main road.

This is a very fine standing stone, almost 4 m high which may well be contemporary with some of the burial mounds around the Loch of Boardhouse, particularly those below Ravie Hill (see no. 68). Local folklore relates that this stone goes down to the loch for drink early on New Year's morning though it must be back in its place by dawn; this is a common folktale told of several stones, sometimes with the additional caution that anyone happening to see the stone in action will not live to celebrate the following New Year.

67 Stone of Setter, Eday

2nd millennium BC.

HY 564371. On the B 9063 some 1.5 km S of Calf Sound, take the minor road NW past Mill Loch; the stone is to the immediate N of the road at the N end of the loch.

Weathering has so furrowed this monolith as to give it a most formidably ancient appearance, enhancing its height (4.5 m) and dominating position overlooking several chambered tombs and Calf Sound to the north (see Eday excursion). Its careful location makes clear the intention of those who set it up that it should become a focal point in the island landscape as viewed from the north and perhaps even from the sea, whence it has certainly taken on the status of a familiar landmark.

The Stane o'Quoybune (Left)

The Stone of Setter

9 DEATH IN EARLY PREHISTORIC TIMES

Inside the tomb at Quoyness, the walls of the chamber soar upwards

People always need shelter but their approach to death is far more variable. The population of Orkney in broch-times must have been extensive, yet there is very little evidence for formal burial in the form of contemporary grave-structures. In contrast, there are many burial mounds and chambered tombs dating from earlier centuries, from around 1000 BC back into the 4th millennium BC. Even if the whole population was not buried in this way, permanent and substantial tombs were certainly considered essential for some members of the community.

Burial mounds and rock carvings

By the early second millennium BC, the practice of cremating human remains and burying them in small pits or stone-lined cists or boxes beneath mounds had been widely adopted in Orkney. Gravegoods are normally few in number and poor in quality (a few sherds of pottery, a steatite bowl or a stone disc would be typical finds from excavations), but there is one outstanding exception in the beautifully decorated gold discs and amber beads from Knowes of Trotty (no. 69). Burial mounds can occur singly or in groups, sometimes large groups as on the north end of the island of Papa Westray, where there are about forty mounds; such groups should be seen as cemeteries and may have remained in use over several centuries. The great ceremonial centre of Brodgar and Stenness (nos 64, 65) acted as a focus for some remarkably large and complex types of barrow, unfortunately dug into long ago with the result that virtually nothing is known of their date and significance.

The fashion for rock art that produced startling great expanses of carving in Argyll seems not to have taken a strong hold in the Northern Isles or in northern mainland Scotland. No carvings on natural rock outcrops have been found in Orkney, but there are two examples of cups and rings carved on detached boulders and re-used at Midhowe (no. 55), which may have originated in the nearby neolithic chambered cairn. More ambitious in concept and technique are the decorative designs carved on earlier neolithic chambered tombs, although only on the Holm of Papa Westray (no. 77) can they be seen in position on the walls of the tomb. The magnificent stone recovered from a destroyed tomb at Pierowall in Westray can be admired in Tankerness House Museum, its carving still beautifully crisp.

A cist excavated at Queenafiold, Twatt, containing a cremation burial and a stone disc

The magnificent carved stone from Pierowall

68 Kirbuster Hill, Barrows

2nd millennium BC.

HY 284263. At Twatt, on the A 986 from Kirkwall to Bisray, take a minor road NNE between the Lochs of Boardhouse and Hundland towards Swannay.

On the gentle south-eastern slopes of Kirbuster Hill is a fine group of at least ten barrows, mostly 6 m to 9 m in diameter, none of which has been excavated. This is one of several barrow cemeteries in the area. Another is visible from the A 987 on the west side of the Loch of Boardhouse, on the very lowest slope of Ravie Hill, where eight mounds can be seen between the road and the loch. It is clear from the hollows in their crests that they have suffered from the 19th-century preoccupation with opening barrows, but the ninth, behind the modern house of Queenafiold, was excavated in the 1960s. The earthen mound had a rough kerb of small stones at its perimeter and a central cist (now rebuilt beside the house); buried in the cist were the cremated remains of an adult male, and adult female and a deer. together with some of the charcoal from the funeral pyre, a sherd of pottery and a stone disc.

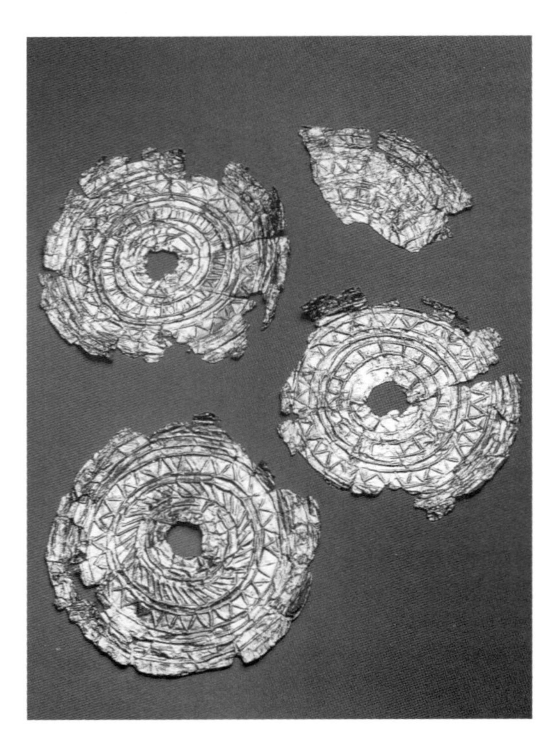

Gold discs from the Knowes of Trotty

69 Knowes of Trotty, Barrows

2nd millennium BC.

HY 342172-342176. On the A 986 some 4 km SE of Dounby, take a minor road leading E towards Evie; after about 2.5 km is the entry to Huntscarth and Netherhouse, and the barrows are S of the latter.

The Ward of Redland is a conspicuous hill, abou 200 m high, and it is noticeable that the barrow builders had no interest in height or maximun visibility, for the mounds are ranged in two row along the foot of the hill. There are eleven earthe mounds, the largest of which is situated closest t the farm of Netherhouse and is about 18 m i diameter and 3 m high; it covered a cist, excavate in 1858, which contained cremated bones and stone slab on which lay four gold discs and 2 amber beads and pendants (these are all in NMS) The thin gold discs are thought to have been cover for buttons, and the technique used in thei decoration links them with goldwork produced i southern England; the gold sheeting has bee hammered on a wooden mound to produc concentric circles of relief decoration. Analysis o the gold itself suggests a Scottish origin, howeve and they may have been the creation of a goldsmit trained in southern England but working i Scotland. The amber was probably imported fron the Baltic, but again via some English source because these particular shapes of bead belong to type of necklace that was made in amber i southern England but in jet normally in Scotland These finds belong to a context in the early 2n millennium BC, and they suggest not only that thi was the first barrow of the group to be raised bu also that it commemorates someone of wealth an high social status.

70 Grice Ness, Cairn, Stronsay

2nd or 3rd millennium BC.

HY 672284. Almost 1.5 km E of Whitehall pier; park at the end of the road and walk E over grasslanc for 500 m.

This neat round mound is easy to spot because it i capped by a modern sea-mark cairn. It is about 1 m in diameter and is surrounded by a low platforn making the whole monument about 21.5 m across. In 1927 the mound, also known as Cutters Tuo, was recorded as conical and 2 m high, which suggests that it is likely to be a bronze-age burial cairn, but there are the tops of several slabs protruding above the turf, and it is possible that these belong to a small chambered cairn rather than to bronze-age cists.

Near the end of the road, at the one place where the ground rises to 10 m OD, there is a wooden pole with footholds for the coastguard to gain a slightly higher view of the east entrance into Papa Sound.

Stronsay's plentiful archaeology is barely understood, for there has been little scientific exploration, but the island was clearly attractive to settlement from early times. There is a long cairn, fully 70 m in length, on Papa Stronsay (one end utilized in the last century by a windmill, the base of which is still visible, HY 668292), and a stalled cairn on Lamb Ness (see no. 54). A rare example of a wooden logboat was found at the edge of Lea Shun loch at the south end of the island in the 19th century, but it was unfortunately allowed to dry out and shrivel.

Houses of the dead

The architectural resemblances between domestic houses and chambered tombs make clear that, in the minds of their builders, tombs were houses of the dead: compare Knap of Howar (no. 63) with Knowe of Yarso (no. 83) and Skara Brae (no. 61) with Maes Howe (no. 72). Their basic designs are related, the shape of the tombs mirroring that of the houses, and floor space is created in the same way - upright slabs divide the Knap of Howar houses into rooms and the chambers of stalled cairns into compartments. Both houses and tombs were long-term, permanent structures used by many generations. Chambered tombs were a combination of the family burial vault and the ossuary, designed to be used over and over again, their entrances sealed between burials. Over the centuries their contents changed, and, even where a tomb has been found intact and scientifically excavated (unfortunately many were disturbed long ago), there can be no telling how much rearrangement or even spring-cleaning has taken place during its lifetime.

The number of burials can vary from single figures to three figures, but they seem to be proportionate

A jumble of bones and skulls in the tomb at Isbister

to the size of tomb, and the fact that men, women and children are represented implies that this was not a special form of burial confined to chieftains. In most cases the skeletons are both disarticulated and very incomplete. At Quanterness (see no. 73) and Isbister (no. 85) the evidence has been attributed to the practice of excarnation (exposing the corpses to natural processes of defleshing before burial in the tomb), but elsewhere, particularly at Midhowe (no. 81), the latest burials were complete articulated skeletons and earlier ones had been sorted and rearranged.

The majority of Orcadian chambered tombs belong to a design known as the Orkney-Cromarty type, prevalent both in Orkney and on the northern mainland of Scotland, in which a passage leads into a chamber divided into compartments by upright slabs; most of the examples described here are stalled cairns, in which the chamber is elongated into as many as the fourteen compartments of Midhowe (no. 81). Some twelve tombs in Orkney belong to the Maes Howe type, in which a passage opens into a large square or rectangular chamber, the walls of which have small entrances into side-cells. It is advisable to take a large torch and water-proof trousers when visiting chambered cairns, for most are dark and many involve crawling on invariably wet floors.

The superb masonry inside the tomb at Cuween

71* Cuween Hill, Chambered Cairn

3rd millennium BC.

HY 364127. On the A 965 Kirkwall to Finstown road, take the signposted minor road just south of Finstown and, after 1 km, a track leading to the house where the key is kept.

Historic Scotland.

You must enter this tomb as did neolithic man uncomfortably on your hands and knees! But it i worth the effort of crawling along the 5.5 m lon passage, not just to see the burial chamber but als to appreciate the psychology behind the design o the tomb and the practical difficulties of an funerary rituals. This is a Maes Howe type o chamber, set within a circular cairn (the roof i modern); the main chamber has four side-cells, on of them double, and the quality of the masonry i very high. Both chamber and cells were cut int solid bedrock and, like Maes Howe, the entrance into the cells are somewhat higher than th chamber floor. When first explored in the 19t century, the skulls of twenty-four dogs were foun on the floor of the chamber, perhaps as a token o tribal identity. There were also the remains of eigh skeletons in the main chamber and cells.

72* Maes Howe, Chambered Cairn

Early 3rd millennium BC.

HY 318127. About 14.5 km WNW of Kirkwall on the A 965; signposted.

Historic Scotland.

More than any other prehistoric monument, th design and execution of Maes Howe epitomises th skill of neolithic masons in Orkney, and the tomb i rightly considered to be one of the suprem achievements of prehistoric Europe. It is inevitabl that such a huge mound should have been robbe long ago, and when it was opened in 1861 by Jame Farrer it was indeed empty of its original contents apart from a fragment of human skull. Its location close to the great ceremonial complex of th

Brodgar-Stenness circles, is presumably no accident.

The mound was built on a levelled circular platform, encircled by a low bank composed of earth scraped up from a shallow ditch on its inner side; the mound itself, 25 m in diameter and 7 m high, consists largely of clay and stones, but there is an inner core of stones casing and supporting the chamber. The outermost part of the entrance-passage has been restored, but from the door-checks inwards it is original. The great boulder in its triangular niche just inside the doorway on the left would have been drawn forwards with ropes to close the entrance. In keeping with the proportions of the tomb, the passage is quite spacious, although at a height of 1.4 m it is not possible to walk upright. Note the enormous slabs with which the passage has been constructed.

The main chamber is about 4.5 m square and was originally about the same height, with three side-cells entered above ground-level; in each corner there is a buttress designed to help in supporting the weight of the corbelled roof. The masonry is superb, the slabs finely adjusted by underpinning or dressing to create a smooth face even where they are in fact oversailing one another towards the roof, and the tapering orthostats facing one side of each buttress not only create an impression of soaring vertical space but attractively interrupt the horizontal lines of the walls.

When Farrer dug into Maes Howe, he found that the chamber had already been broken into, as he did, from the top; from *Orkneyinga Saga* and from the runic inscriptions on the walls of the chamber, it is clear that it was entered on more than one occasion by Norsemen in the 12th century, to whom the mound was known as *Orkhaugr*. During the struggle between the rival earls Erlend and Harald for control of the earldom, Harald and some of his men sought shelter in Maes Howe from a snowstorm, but it was such a terrible experience that two of them went mad, `which slowed them down badly' says the saga, though they still reached their destination by nightfall. The following winter of 1153-4, crusaders gathered together ready for a trip to the Holy Land broke into the chamber and incised some of the runic inscriptions, and there were probably other occasions as well when runes

Maes Howe from the air (Top)

The entrance passage into Maes Howe (Middle)

Inside Maes Howe, small cells open off the spacious chamber (Bottom)

Maes Howe dragon

Runic inscription No. 18 on north side of entrance to south-east cell (Top right)

were cut there. This is one of the largest extant collection of runic inscriptions carved in stone. There are about thirty inscriptions, including both ordinary runes and cryptographic twig runes, and there are also some beautifully executed carvings of a walrus, a serpent knot and a dragon or lion on the north-east buttress, all in typically vigorous Scandinavian style.

Two of the most interesting inscriptions are nos 18 and 16 (the original numbering applied by Farrer is still used) on the large block on the north side of the entrance to the south-east cell and continuing on the cell lintel, which read, in a mixture of twig runes and ordinary runes: `These runes were carved by the man most skilled in runes in the western ocean', `with the axe which belonged to Gaukr Trandilsson in the south of Iceland'. A superb piece of genealogical detective work by a modern Icelander, Hermann Palsson, has identified the rune-carver as Thorhallr Asgrimsson, the great-great-great grandson of the man who slew Gaukr Trandilsson some 200 years earlier, the story of which is told in *Njals Saga*. For the archaeologist trying to use objects as dating evidence, the thought of an axe still in use after six generations very sobering!

Several other inscriptions mention treasure: eg `It long ago that a great treasure was hidden here `Happy is he who might find the great treasure Until recently, it was assumed that this was wishf thinking and no more, as treasure to Norseme would mean gold or silver, neither of which coul have been buried with the original pre-met neolithic occupants of the tomb. A new slant to th question arose after excavations in the 1970s, whe structural evidence for a rebuilding of the bar encircling the mound was radiocarbon dated to th 9th century AD. It now seems possible that th tomb was re-used and its external appearanc improved for the burial of a Viking chieftain, who rich grave-goods were stolen three centuries late `Hakon alone bore the treasure out of this moun records one of the inscriptions, while anoth insists `It is certain and true as I say, that th treasure has been moved from here. The treasu was taken away three nights before they broke int his mound'.

3 Wideford Hill, Chambered Cairn

·d millennium BC.

Y 409121. Take the A 965 from Kirkwall towards ·nstown for almost 8 km, then a signposted minor ·ad SE for 2.5 km (this is e simplest rather than the quickest route); signposted footpath leads N over rough moorland ·r 1.5 km.

storic Scotland.

hough not an easy walk, the reward is a tomb in ·cellent condition and, on a clear day, a beautiful ·ew over the Bay of Firth. This is another Maes owe design and, as at Quoyness (no. 84), all three all-faces are visible, representing the various ages of construction of the cairn. The chamber ith its three side-cells is dug back into the hillside ·d the entrance is downslope (although entry is ·w through a hatch in the roof, the original ·ssage being only 0.6 m high). Excavation in the ·th century found the cells to be empty, although e main chamber has been deliberately filled with ·bble.

On the northern lower slope of Wideford at Quanterness (HY 417129), there is a large mound which, though inaccessible, contains a magnificent tomb of Maes Howe design, with six cells opening off the main chamber. Recent excavation of 80% of the tomb (the rest left deliberately for posterity) yielded human bones estimated to belong to 157 individuals, who had been brought into the tomb in skeletal state as at Isbister (no. 85). Unlike Wideford the tomb had not been closed by infilling. Radiocarbon dates indicate that Quanterness was built around 3400 BC and remained in use for about a thousand years.

The long chamber at Unstan is divided into burial compartments by upright slabs, and a small cell opens to the left

Inside the chamber at Wideford

(Top left)

74* Unstan, Chambered Cairn

3rd millennium BC.

HY 282117. Just N of the A 965 some 4 km NE of Stromness; signposted.

Historic Scotland.

This is the stalled cairn after which Unstan Ware was named, for its excavation in the late 19th century yielded sherds of at least thirty-five bowls of this distinctively shaped and decorated ware. It was built on a low-lying promontory on the south shore of the Loch of Stenness.

The circular cairn covers a chamber very similar to that at Isbister (no. 85): it is divided by upright slabs into three central compartments and two shelved end-cells, and a side-cell opens off the west wall of the central compartment. The lintel over the cell bears a brief runic inscription, but the stone is not in its original position (having been placed here during restoration); the fact that the runes are carved across the narrow face of the slab implies that it was once set upright. The bird and other doodles on the same slab have apparently been added since restoration this century.

Beyond the tomb, two lines of rampart and ditch cut off the tip of the promontory; nothing is known of the date of this fortified enclosure, an unusual monument for the Northern Isles, and it is not inconceivable that it might be neolithic.

Truly megalithic building inside the Vinquoy tomb

Plan of Vinquoy
(Bottom right)

75 Vinquoy, Chambered Cairn, Eday

3rd millennium BC.

HY 560381. On Vinquoy Hill at the N end of the island; from the B 9063, take the minor road NW past Mill Loch for about 1.5 km and walk NNE along the ridge for about 0.5km.

Orkney Islands Council.

Set on a hilltop, this tomb commands a very extensive view over Orkney. It is a well-preserved and restored example of a Maes Howe type of tomb, with a main chamber and four side-cells. As it was built on a slope, the tomb is partly subterranean, with its entrance downslope and a level floor created by digging back into the hillside. The main chamber must originally have been at least 3 m high, and the corbelling of its roof cannot have been an easy task given the irregular fracturing of the local stone.

Nothing is known of the original contents of the tomb.

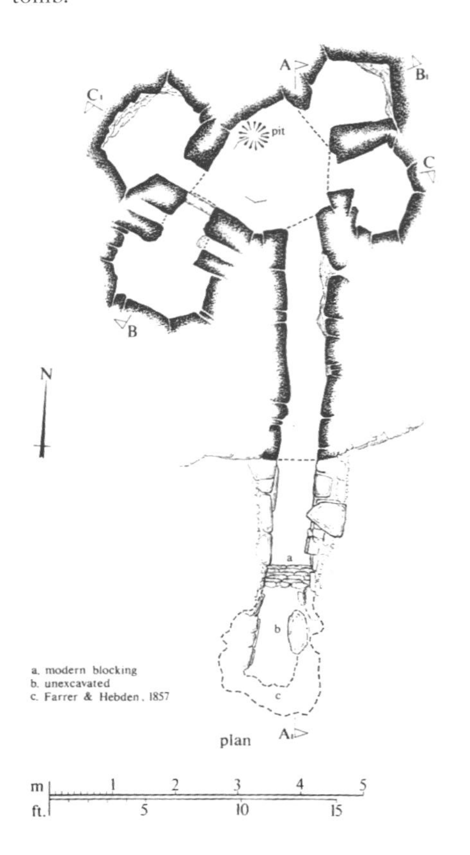

76 Calf of Eday Long, Chambered Cairn, Eday

4th and 3rd millennia BC.

HY 578386. There is a boat service available on request from Calfsound in Eday to the Calf of Eday; see Eday excursion for monuments on the Calf.

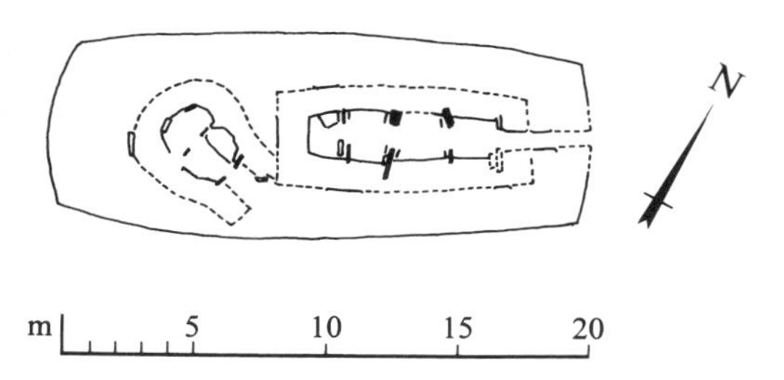

This large cairn was excavated in 1936 and, although ruinous and overgrown, the two chambers are still visible. This is a multi-period monument and very similar in its development to Holm of Papa Westray North (no. 78). The earliest tomb was small and consisted of two compartments within a small cairn. At some later stage (the detailed chronology is unknown), a larger stalled tomb was built to the immediate east, within its own rectangular cairn. Finally, both chambers and their cairns were enclosed within a larger rectangular cairn, maintaining the entrance passage into the eastern tomb. Sherds of Unstan pottery, flint tools and two stones axes were recovered from the stalled chamber, but soil conditions were unsuited to the recovery of bones, with the result that the number of burials is unknown.

On the slope just east of the cairn are the ruins of an iron-age domestic settlement, and the two smaller tombs nearby are almost intact and can be entered, although very little is known of their history or contents.

77 Holm of Papa Westray South, Chambered Cairn, Papa Westray

3rd millennium BC.

HY 509518. At the S end of the Holm, a small island off the E coast of Papa Westray; enquire at the Papay Community Co-operative for a boat.

Historic Scotland.

Although officially known as Papa Westray, the island is locally called Papay.

It is likely that, in neolithic times, Holm of Papay was not an island but a promontory attached at the north end to Papa Westray, but even so it must be regarded as an uncommonly remote place to find one of the largest and most extraordinary tombs in Orkney. It is essentially a Maes Howe design, with side-cells opening off a main rectangular chamber, but the enclosing cairn is oblong rather than round simply as the most economic way to encompass an enormously elongated chamber, fully 20.5 m in length. The entrance-passage opens into the south-east long side of the chamber and, perhaps as a measure to strengthen the roof, there is a sub-dividing wall at either end of the chamber, each with a low doorway to allow access. No fewer than twelve side-cells, two of them double, are ranged round the chamber, all of them intact with lintelled entrances only 40 cm to 60 cm high.

Plan showing the two chambers at Calf of Eday Long (Left)

The roof over the main chamber is modern, and the visitor enters through a hatch and down a ladder rather than through the original low passage,

Plan of the huge tomb at Holm of Papa Westray South

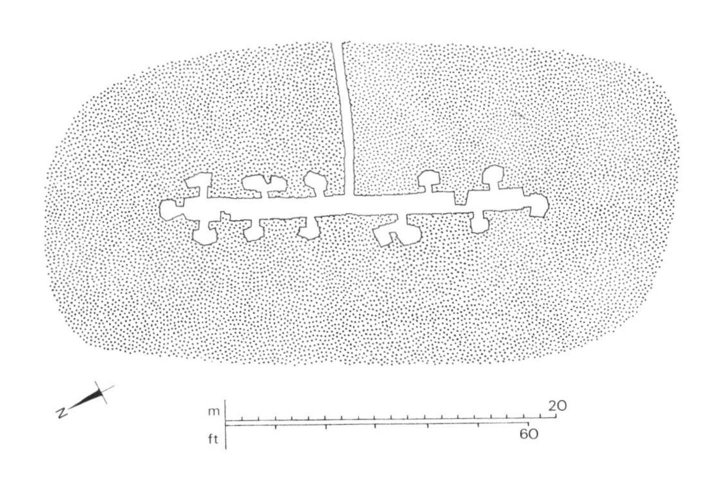

Decoration above a side-cell in Holm of Papa Westray South

Holm of Papa Westray South: inside the long chamber with a massive lintel over the entrance into one of the end-chambers

although it is still complete. There are decorative carvings to discover, one on the south-east wall of the central part of the chamber, just south of the entrance, consisting of a double ring and an inverted V-motif, and three at the south-west end of the chamber, beyond the dividing wall; on the lintel over the entrance to the south-east cell there are pecked dots and arcs, some combined to make 'eye-brow' motifs which are also to be found in Irish chambered tombs, and on the opposite wall are zig-zag and circle motifs. Nothing is known of the original contents of the tomb.

78 Holm of Papa Westray North, Papa Westray

c 3200 BC.

HY 504522.

At the north end of the island.

This stalled cairn was excavated in the 1980s and, although largely filled in again as a protective measure, the main features of the tomb are still visible (the outer wall-face was built up so that the original walling is safely beneath ground-level). The cairn is rectangular with a passage at the north end leading into a rectangular chamber, subdivided by upright slabs into four compartments. At the far end of the chamber is a small cell, which was apparently the first structure to be built and which was sealed off during the use of the main chamber. After it was sealed, a small stone box was constructed in the end-compartment, and this was found to be full of very small fishbones, perhaps reflecting some part of the ceremonies surrounding burial in the tomb. Fishing has always been part of the local economy, supplementing the fruits of the

The entrance passage and stalled chamber as excavated at Holm of Papa Westray North (Right)

land. Bones from a small number of people remained in the tomb, both adults and children, and there was broken pottery and food refuse on the floor. After the final burial, the roof was removed and the entire tomb was filled with earth and stones.

Traces of ancient field-walls and small cairns can be seen to the south and east of the tomb.

79 Dwarfie Stane, Rock-cut Tomb, Hoy

3rd millennium BC.

HY 243004. The ferry from Stromness lands at Moa Ness on the NE coast of the island; take the B 9049 S for 2 km and then the minor road S towards Rackwick for another 2 km. The site is visible on the hillside to the S of the road; signposted.

Historic Scotland.

As the only chambered tomb known on Hoy, it is perhaps fitting that the Dwarfie Stane should be an oddity. Its builders, or rather carvers, used a huge isolated natural block of sandstone to hollow out of the solid rock a small chamber, with two side-cells entered over projecting sills. A large boulder lying outside the entrance is the original blocking stone, which is recorded as having been seen in position in the 16th century, but nothing is known of the contents of the tomb. Hollowing out this tomb must have been a gruelling task for just a few people at a time, and the marks of their stone tools can be seen on the roof of the south cell.

This is the only rock-cut tomb in Britain, but the construction of other Orcadian tombs has involved cutting into bedrock (eg Cuween, no. 71), and at Sand Fiold near Skara Brae an extraordinary cist was built within a rock-cut pit. The Dwarfie Stane has always caught the imagination of visitors, including Sir Walter Scott who incorporated it into his novel *The Pirate*. The earliest of the many names carved on the tomb is that of H Ross in 1735, but the most intriguing is that of Major W Mouncey who in 1850 not only carved his name in Latin backwards but added an inscription in exquisite Persian calligraphy to the effect that 'I have sat two nights and so learnt patience'.

The extraordinary rock-cut Dwarfie Stane (Top)

Major Mouncey's graffiti

Major Mouncey was a former British spy in Persia, but it is thought that his ordeal at the Dwarfie Stane may have been caused by midges rather than anything more sinister.

80 Blackhammer, Chambered Tomb, Rousay

HY 414276. Signposted to the N of the B 9064.

Historic Scotland.

Another well-preserved stalled cairn, known as Blackhammer, is set on a terrace below the Knowe of Yarso (no. 83). The entrance passage opens from the side of the oblong cairn, but access for the modern visitor is by ladder through the roof. The builders of the tomb created a decorative appearance by setting the stones of the outer wall-face slanting to form alternate triangles, and this can still be seen on either side of the entrance. When the passage was sealed for the last time, again stones were set flush with the outer wall and matching the slant of the stones on either side.

The chamber has seven compartments, although at some later date rough stonework has been inserted into the central compartment and four of the dividing slabs are missing. The tomb was excavated in 1936, and the partial remains of one person were found in the westernmost compartment and those of another in the entrance passage. There were also animal bones, especially sheep, along with pottery, flint tools, part of a bone pin and a stone axe.

To the west are the grass-grown remains of a very long stalled cairn, Knowe of Ramsay (HY 400279), which on excavation proved to contain a chamber divided into fourteen compartments, entered from the south-east end.

81 Midhowe, Chambered Cairn, Rousay

3rd millennium BC.

HY 372304. Take the B 9064 from Trumland to a point about 2 km beyond the Westness where the footpath to Midhowe broch and cairn is signposted.

Historic Scotland.

Built on low-lying ground near the sea, this excavated stalled cairn is entirely housed within a modern hangar-like building, so that it can be viewed both at ground-level and from an overhead walkway; it is a very fine monument, with an elongated chamber, 23 m in length, divided by pairs of upright slabs into twelve compartments and encased within an oblong cairn. A decorative effect has been achieved on the outer face of the cairn by setting stones at an angle, best seen almost as a herring-bone pattern on the east face. At its north-east corners, the cairn is attached to contemporary field-walls which have been traced for about 20 m and 13 m respectively, underlining the association of the tomb with its surrounding agrarian landscape.

The chamber had been filled with stones when the tomb was closed (masonry closing the passage is still in position) and the contents were undisturbed: remains of twenty-five people were found, mostly lying on or tucked beneath the shelves along the east side of the chamber, including nine complete skeletons.

The stalled chamber at Midhowe

82 Taversoe Tuick, Chambered Cairn, Rousay

3rd millennium BC.

HY 425276. Just N of the B 9064, some 1 km from the pier; signposted.

Historic Scotland.

This is one of two Orcadian tombs remarkable for their double-storey design; the other is Huntersquoy on Eday (HY 562377) of which little can now be seen. In both cases, there is an upper and a lower chamber, each with its own entrance-passage opening in diametrically opposed directions and with no access between the two, so that they are in effect two separate tombs although they appear to have been built simultaneously. At Taversoe Tuick it is possible to enter both chambers, and to look into an unusual miniature 'tomb' built at the edge of the platform on which the main tomb stands, close close to the passage leading into the lower chamber. It contained three pottery bowls and may have been connected with ritual activities.

83 Knowe of Yarso, Chambered Cairn, Rousay

3rd millennium.

HY 404279. Take the B 9064 from Trumland W for 2.5 km, where a signposted path leads uphill from the road to the tomb.

Historic Scotland.

The builders of this tomb chose a terrace on a steep hillside with a superb view over Eynhallow Sound, regardless of the effort involved in carrying up the slabs used in its construction. It has a stalled chamber set within a sub-rectangular cairn, and a decorative effect was achieved in the outer wall-face by setting the slabs at an angle. The chamber is protected by a modern roof, and its walls are well-preserved to a height of about 1.8 m (see p.41); it is divided into three compartments, the end one double-sized but nonetheless marked off into two areas by low upright slabs. Parts of twenty-nine individuals were found in the chamber, mostly in the innermost compartment, the skulls carefully arranged against the wall, and amongst the animal bones were remains of some thirty-six deer. There was also an unusually large number of flint tools,

The lower chamber at Taversoe Tuick

especially scrapers, which may perhaps be connected symbolically with the deer in the sense of being tools suitable for the preparation of animal skins for clothing and other articles.

84 Quoyness, Chambered Cairn, Sanday

3rd millennium BC.

HY 676377. Sanday can be reached by sea or air from Kirkwall; the tomb is on the Els Ness peninsula, some 6 km from Kettletoft via the B 9069 and signposted footpath.

Historic Scotland.

The reconstructed entrance into the tomb at Quoyness

The location of Quoyness is very similar to that of Holm of Papa Westray South (no. 77), on an isolated peninsula, except that Els Ness, unlike the Holm of Papay, is still, just, connected to the adjacent mainland. Both are outstanding examples of Maes Howe type tombs. Although lacking its original roof, the chamber stands intact to its full height of 4 m, and consequently the external appearance of the cairn is also very impressive, the more so as it stands on an artificial platform. Three consecutive wall-faces can be seen, representing the inner cairn round the chamber, a middle revetment flush with the outer end of the entrance-passage and an outer casing. Originally the entrance-passage was roofed for its full length of 9 m, but only the inner 3.5 m is now intact and roofed at a height of 0.6 m - the complete 9 m crawl must have been a daunting experience!

Emerging on hands and knees, the chamber seems vast and soaring skywards. Low entrances open into six side-cells, all but two of which contained burials, and there were further burials in a cist sunk into a pit in the southern corner of the chamber. Unfortunately this was a depressingly bad 19th-century excavation in which an enormous amount of archaeological information was lost. Objects found in and around the tomb included bone and stone implements similar to examples from the contemporary settlement as Skara Brae (no. 61), and it is likely that the tomb was built very early in the 3rd millennium BC.

The wrecked but still impressive mound nearby to the south may well have been another chambered tomb, traditionally known as Egmondshowe (HY 676375); it is enclosed by an arc of eleven small bronze-age burial mounds connected by a bank. At least another twenty-six small cairns are scattered over the peninsula, implying its continuing sanctity as a burial place throughout the 2nd millennium BC. The excavation of Tofts Ness (no. 60) has shown, however, that sometimes such cairns are the result of domestic rather than funerary use.

85 Isbister, Chambered Cairn, South Ronaldsay

3rd-late 4th millennium.

ND 470845. Take the A 961 from Kirkwall to its terminus at the S end of South Ronaldsay, turn E on the B 9041 for 1.5 km and then the signposted minor road S to Liddle Farm.

Orkney Islands Council.

Like the burnt mound at Liddle (no. 59), the Isbister tomb is owned, and indeed was excavated, by the farmer, Mr R Simison, and there is a small display of finds at the farm, where visitors will be directed or taken to the tomb. The cairn is oval, though its shape is somewhat obscured by later additions, and the entrance to the chamber faces out to sea; the tomb is now quite close to precipitous cliffs and, even allowing for erosion, its situation must always have been spectacular.

Entrance passage and side-cell at Isbister

The roof of the chamber had been removed in antiquity when the tomb was filled with stones and earth after the final burials, but there is now a modern roof. The design of the tomb shows it to be

Isbister tomb during excavation

a hybrid, a stalled cairn furnished with side-cells in the manner of the Maes Howe type; the main chamber is divided into three compartments by pairs of upright slabs, and there are three side-cells and a shelved compartment at either end of the chamber, making an overall length of just over 8 m. Apart from the northern end-cell and the north-east side-cell, which had been disturbed and robbed prior to the excavation, the rest of the tomb and its contents were intact, and the floor deposits yielded many human and animal bones and fishbones. The two western side-cells had been used primarily for human skulls. Particularly intriguing was the inclusion of carcases and talons of sea-eagles, perhaps a totemistic feature comparable to the dog skulls at Cuween (no.71) and the fishbones at Holm of Papa Westray North (no. 78), and Isbister has become popularly known as the Tomb of the Eagles. Analysis of the human bones suggests that around 340 people were buried in the tomb, though many individuals were represented by very few bones. It has been suggested that the bodies were excarnated elsewhere, and token deposits of bones taken into the tomb. A large amount of sherds from Unstan Ware bowls was also found in the tomb, mostly in a pile in the main chamber opposite the entrance. A series of radiocarbon dates indicates a very long period of use for the tomb of around 800 years after its construction in about 3000 BC.

86 Point of Cott, Chambered Cairn, Westray

HY 465474. About 4 km SE of Pierowall on the B 9066, take a minor road N at HY 463458; park out of the way of farm traffic and walk NE to the coast.

Before it was excavated in the 1980s, this was an eroding long cairn some 1.5 m high, which had once been more than 30 m long. Fears that coastal erosion would destroy it completely led to its excavation, but the basal course of the structures uncovered is still visible, if overgrown. This must have been a magnificent sight when it was in use, for the cairn curved outwards on either side of the entrance to form long horns, thus creating a spacious forecourt in front of the tomb facade. The entrance passage was still roofed with slabs set on edge, but the long stalled chamber was roofless. It was divided into four compartments, of which the innermost was furnished by a double box formed of low upright slabs. The partial remains of twelve people were recovered, both adults and children, along with pottery and animal bones.

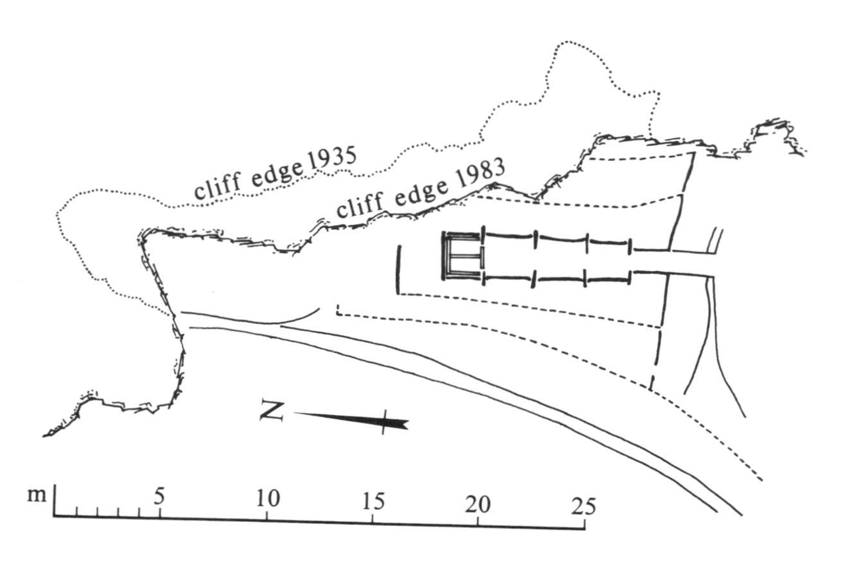

Plan of stalled cairn at Point of Cott

MUSEUMS AND VISITOR CENTRES

There are small displays of artefacts in site museums at Skara Brae (no. 61) and Isbister (no. 85), and the broch of Gurness has a more extensive visitor centre (no. 53). A general display on Orcadian prehistory may be seen at Tormiston Mill (no. 26).

Corrigall Farm Museum, see no. 23.

Kirbuster Farm Museum, see no. 25.

Scapa Flow Visitor Centre, Lyness, Hoy, see no. 4.

Stromness Museum, Alfred Street, Stromness, is primarily a natural history and maritime museum, including the naval history of Scapa Flow.

Tankerness House Museum, Broad Street, Kirkwall, a fine 16th-century house (no. 20), contains major archaeological collections, including finds from Skara Brae, Gurness, Skaill and Scar, the neolithic carved stone from Pierowall and the Pictish symbol stone from Knowe of Burrian.

The garden courtyard at Kirbuster Farm Museum

View across Westray from the top of Noltland Castle

BIBLIOGRAPHY

Anderson, PD *Black Patie: the life and times of Patrick Stewart, Earl of Orkney, Lord of Shetland*, Edinburgh, 1992.

Aslet, C *The Last Country Houses*, New Haven & London, 1982.

Batey, CE, Jesch, J and Morris, CD *The Viking Age in Caithness, Orkney and the North Atlantic*, Edinburgh, 1993.

Berry, RJ and Firth, HN (eds) *The People of Orkney*, Kirkwall, 1986.

Burgher, L *Orkney: an illustrated architectural guide*, Edinburgh, 1991.

Crawford, BE *Scandinavian Scotland*, Leicester, 1987.

Crawford, BE (ed) *St Magnus Cathedral and Orkney's Twelfth Century Renaissance*, Aberdeen, 1988.

Cruden, S *The Scottish Castle*, Edinburgh, 1960.

Davidson, JL and Henshall, AS *The Chambered Cairns of Orkney*, Edinburgh, 1989.

Donaldson, G *A Northern Commonwealth: Scotland and Norway*, Edinburgh, 1990.

Dunbar, JG *The Historic Architecture of Scotland*, London, 2nd edition 1978.

Fawcett, R *Scottish Medieval Churches*, Edinburgh, 1985.

Fenton, A *The Northern Isles: Orkney and Shetland*, Edinburgh, 1978.

Fenton, A & Palsson, H (eds) *The Northern and Western Isles in the Viking World*, Edinburgh, 1984.

Foster, SM *Picts, Gaels and Scots*, London, 1996.

Garnham, T *Melsetter House: William Richard Lethaby*, London, 1993.

Gifford, J *Highland and Islands*, London, 1992.

Hedges, J *Tomb of the Eagles*, London, 1984.

Hedges, JW *A Guide to Isbister Chambered Tomb and Liddle Burnt Mound, South Ronaldsay, Orkney*, Oxford, 1985.

Hewison, WS *This Great Harbour - Scapa Flow*, Kirkwall, 1985.

Hunter, JR *Rescue Excavations on the Brough of Birsay 1974-82*, Edinburgh, 1986.

Hume, JR *The Industrial Monuments of Scotland, 2 The Highlands & Islands*, London, 1977.

Miller, R *Orkney*, London, 1976.

Morris, CD *The Birsay Bay Project, vol 1, Brough Road Excavations 1976-1982*, Durham, 1989.

Munro, RW *Scottish Lighthouses*, Stornoway, 1979.

Orkney Heritage, *vol. 2, Birsay: a centre of political and ecclesiastical power*, Kirkwall, 1983.

Palsson, H & Edwards, P *Orkneyinga Saga*, London, 1978.

Rendall, J *Papay: a guide to places of interest*, Papa Westray, 1992.

Renfrew, C (ed) *The Prehistory of Orkney*, Edinburgh, 1985.

Ritchie, A *Picts*, Edinburgh, 1989.

Ritchie, A *Viking Scotland*, London, 1993.

Ritchie, A *Prehistoric Orkney*, London, 1995.

Ritchie, A & Ritchie, G *The Ancient Monuments of Orkney*, Edinburgh, 1995.

Ritchie, JNG *Brochs of Scotland*, Aylesbury, 1988.

Ritchie, G & Ritchie, A *Scotland: Archaeology and Early History*, Edinburgh, 1991.

Royal Commission on the Ancient and Historical Monuments of Scotland *An Inventory of the Ancient and Historical Monuments of Orkney and Shetland*, Edinburgh, 1946.

Schrank, G *An Orkney Estate: improvements at Graemeshall, 1827-1888*, East Linton, 1995.

Scott, Sir Walter *Northern Lights*, Hawick, 1982.

Tabraham, C *Scottish Castles and Fortifications*, Edinburgh, 1986.

Thomson, WPL *The Little General and the Rousay Crofters: crisis and conflict on an Orkney estate*, Edinburgh, 1981.

Thomson, WPL *Kelp-making in Orkney*, Kirkwall, 1983.

Thomson, WPL *History of Orkney*, Edinburgh, 1987.

Wainwright, FT (ed) *The Northern Isles*, London, 1962.

There are also guide booklets or leaflets to individual monuments in the care of Historic Scotland: Brough of Birsay, Dounby Click Mill, the Earl's and Bishop's Palaces in Kirkwall, Gurness, Maes Howe, Noltland Castle and Skara Brae.

The north aisle of the choir of St Magnus Cathedral

INDEX OF PLACES

Printed in Scotland for The Stationery Office Ltd by (3808)
Dd 293084 C50 10/96